WITHDRAWN

LIBRARY SERVICES TO THE HANDICAPPED
Maine State Library
Augusta, Maine   04330

non fee

FOLIAGE PLANTS
FOR YOUR GARDEN

FOLIAGE PLANTS
FOR YOUR GARDEN

By

DOUGLAS BARTRUM

MAGNA PRINT BOOKS
LITTON . YORKSHIRE

SEP 1 3 1976

LARGE TYPE EDITION

635.975
B294f

First Published in large print 1975
by
Magna Print Books
Litton, Skipton, Yorkshire
by arrangement with
W. & G. Foyle Limited
London

© Large Print Edition 1975
Magna Print Books

ISBN 0 86009 038 8

Printed in Great Britain

Contents

Introduction

THE beautifully divided *Acanthus* leaf fired the imagination of the early Greek architects. Acanthus leaves and scrolls are a characteristic feature of the carving on the Corinthian capitals of the monuments and temples dating about 400 B.C. (*See Fig. 1.*)

We grow the plant in our gardens (it was probably *Acanthus spinosus,* a native of Southern Europe) and admire it as much for its foliage as for its flowers. In fact before it comes into bloom in summer it makes a handsome foliage plant, with its finely cut leaves — about eight spiny segments to each leaf. The flower-spikes are by no means arresting and it is a good plan to cut them off when they fade, otherwise they detract from the beauty of the foliage for the rest of the year.

Owen Jones in *The Grammar of Ornament* gives a reproduction from a photograph of the leaf and says, "In the use of the Acanthus leaf the Romans showed but little art. They received it from the Greeks beautifully conventionalised; they went much nearer to the general outline, but exaggerated the surface-decoration. The Greeks confined themselves to expressing the principle of the foliation of the leaf, and bestowed all their care in the delicate undulations of its surface." (*See Fig. 2.*)

The leaves of many plants have a sculptural quality which delights the eye and amply satisfies it; and the flowers of some (as those of *Hosta glauca*) seem superfluous.

Other plants we grow for their foliage have flowers which are insignificant and even quite ugly — the dull white, rather dirty-looking corymbs of *Cassinia fulvida,* for example; and *Santolina chamaecyparissus,* the well-known silver-white Lavender Cotton, has a redundancy of tiny yellow heads. Most gardeners rightly cut them off as soon as they begin to show.

Another, *Senecio greyii* (*S. Laxifolius*), with grey leaves, white-felted underneath, also has small yellow flowers in the summer, which many people clip off before they open. Their vivid yellow contrasts rather too strongly with the soft grey-white leaves. It is a hard, staring colour; the leaves are much more attractive.

8

The *Hosta* flowers, lily-like, pale, washy mauve ones, I leave, because they soon fade and they are not showy. After about a fortnight, when the seeds begin to form, I cut the stems off at a point just below the leaves. Many flowers of foliage plants have just as short a blooming period; the leaves last much longer; we have them for perhaps nine months of the year.

On the other hand, the flowers of some are striking; for instance, in the Ornamental Rhubarb, *Rheum* 'Bowles' Crimson'; they come in crimson panicles on tall stems and for a few weeks eclipse the beauty of the leaves.

Similarly, in *Bergenia (Saxifraga) ligulata,* a plant often seen in gardens, the pink flowers, in thick clusters on fleshy stems, are beautiful for several weeks during early spring. But the broad, round leaves touching the ground are attractive for many months.

In some plants we grow for their foliage, the flowers are scarcely noticeable, in the alpine *Thymus pseudolanuginosus,* for example. I don't ever remember seeing them bloom; this particular plant actually has very few. It has, incidentally, a very pleasant smell; by patting the soft mass of grey, woolly foliage with the palm of your hand you bring it out strongly.

A similar plant is the common Southernwood (*Artemisia abrotanum*): its flower-heads are a dull yellow and inconspicuous among the dense, finely cut aromatic foliage.

In some species of *Euphorbia,* the flowers are yellowish-green, tiny and surrounded by small leaves the same colour, which come from the top of the stems in spring. In *E. epithymoides* we get a delightful combination of dark, almost blue, green leaves on the stems, and above them the light yellow-green of the leafy inflorescence.

The exotic-looking *Yucca* is another type of foliage plant — we can call it a foliage plant, for it often doesn't flower at all freely in many of our gardens. With its stiff, sword-like leaves, it is a plant that needs careful placing — it is not at all suitable for the herbaceous border, and I don't like to see it associated with shrubs. And there is no room for it in a small garden. But it is most arresting massed in a group of a dozen or more, whether it flowers or not.

Vegetables? The Beetroot (*Beta vulgaris*) is often used. No doubt you will have seen it planted out in formal flower-beds, its red-bronze leaves providing some charming foliage effects; it is especially lovely as a background to the carpeting sky-blue Lobelia. The Spinach (*Spinacia oleracea*) is occasionally used in formal beds. Its shining green leaves, with conspicuous white mid-ribs, resemble those of the noble *Lysichitum americanum,* a bog or waterside plant which has leaves often two and a half feet long and one foot wide, and large lemon-yellow Arum-like flowers.

The Globe Artichoke (*Cynara scolymus*) is a glorious Silver Thistle, decorative wherever it is grown. Find room for one in the herbaceous border.

There are some very decorative varieties of the Spinach Beet, viz. *Beta vulgaris* var. *cruenta,* which has large leaves, red or green, with yellow mid-ribs; the colouring is garish; it doesn't appeal to everybody. Var. Victoria has glistening deep red leaves. These are specifically ornamental foliage plants which are valuable in borders and beds and for sub-tropical garden effects. They are best treated as biennials. (The fleshy roots may be cooked and make delicious vegetables.)

The Cabbages or Kales are more rarely seen, although when they are given an appropriate setting, say, amongst other foliage plants on the sloping bank of a stream or a pond, the taller Kales create a singularly graceful effect with their curly, mauvish green leaves surmounted, for a few weeks, with erect racemes of pale yellow flowers. Or they might be used for contrast among tall plants in the herbaceous border. There are different varieties of Kales grown in a show-bed at the University Botanic Garden, Oxford.

And from the plebeian vegetable to the truly exotic foliage plants of the hothouse, which are sometimes used in our gardens during mid-summer. They are left in their pots as a rule and sunk in the soil, then lifted and housed as soon as the weather turns cold.

Begonia rex (a native of Assam, India) and its many varieties are special favourites with gardeners. These are remarkably ornamental foliage plants, with oval, wrinkled leaves, beautifully marked with silver and green, red and green, purple and green: the colouring varies enormously in the different kinds raised from the type plant. They should not be planted out before June.

There are Ferns, wild, cultivated and exotic rare ones that can be brought outside from the greenhouse; and Grasses, some of which look as artificial as the vividly coloured Begonias. The Ferns, flowerless, pre-eminently foliage plants, are graceful and cool-looking with their finely cut leaves; and the grasses — annual and perennial kinds may be grown — are remarkable for their variety of form and colouring. *Festuca ovina glauca* is a dwarf glaucous-blue perennial grass which is attractive and pleasant to see all through the winter. No border or bed need be completely bare during the autumn and winter if some of these ornamental perennial kinds are grown. Many are small enough for pots: the Blue Festuca mentioned above, for instance.

Bamboos for tropical effects are usually reserved for the biggest gardens; they are some of the wildest of spreaders and soon cover large areas. There is an enormous variety; most of them will thrive in ordinary soils and do not need boggy conditions. They are eminently suitable for the wild garden, where they may be used effectively in wide sweeps or bold groupings; and they are in perfect harmony with water — on the sloping banks of a pool or edging a stream.

Then there are the foliage-aquatics, the floating plants like the Water-lilies, whose flat leaves, lovely green or reddish bronze, are beautiful even without the flowers; the big-leaved Gunneras and, in contrast with them, the tall, slender rushes.

We don't look for fragrance in foliage plants on the whole, but many have a delightful aroma: the Southernwood is perhaps the best known; the Santolinas are also aromatic. These plants haven't the rich scents of flowers, but their pungent smell is always refreshing.

All-green gardens or foliage gardens are rare in this country; but they are common in Japan. Mrs. Basil Taylor describes these Green Gardens in her book *Japanese Gardens* and gives a coloured plate of the Kuradani Temple Garden, Kyoto, on the Island of Honshu. The shades of green — of the grass, the low clipped shrubs, the Hosta-like plants massed in the foreground — give the garden a look of repose and serenity.

An all-green garden can be a garden within a garden: a feature more valuable, I consider, than the herbaceous border or the rockery.

In the following chapters different ways of using foliage plants are described. For my part, I like to see many of them set in some isolated position where they can display their beauty to the full. A broad-leaved Hosta, for instance, planted on the bend of a pathway or on the edge of a pool.

CHAPTER I

The Foliage Garden

A FOLIAGE garden or a Green Garden can be part of a garden, as I have already stated: a feature like the rockery, although this would probably be smaller. For the foliage garden must be big enough to walk through; and a rockery often takes up no more room than a short, narrow flower-border — at least in areas of half an acre or so.

A foliage garden must be a shady place, where we can sit and relax and enjoy our leisure moments quietly. A site then where trees are growing is ideal. And for a small garden a dozen different sorts of foliage plants should be enough.

Diversity is provided mainly by form: the broad, spreading leaf of the Hosta; the finely cut leaf of the Ferns; the ornamental Grasses; and there are many other types which I have touched upon in the introduction. Vividly coloured plants, however, will not be wanted.

The lay-out depends on the contours of the ground and on the site chosen. A dell or a gentle slope has more possibilites than a flat piece of ground. It needs bounding by trees and shrubs. I think, to cut it off from the garden proper. A winding grass pathway not less than four feet wide with a sloping bank in the background, at the top of which evergreen shrubs are growing, is an admirable foundation to work on. (If you are going to sow the grass seed, choose a good variety such as Carter's 'Shaded Lawn', a tested seed suitable for under trees and shady places and of a fresh green colour.)

First, the extraneous ornament: rock or stone, which includes flag-stones, and water are used. These are seen to best advantage, of course, in large gardens.

Three or four thick blocks of flat stone should be sunk in the ground, with a couple of inches protruding, and lead like stepping-stones to a pool, which need not be more than four feet in diameter. Grass must be planted round the stones and clipped over occasionally to keep it reasonably short.

Near the water plant a group of Hostas; few things look as lovely against a pool as the Hosta, with its cool-looking, beautifully shaped leaves. There are many species from which to choose: for the small pool I have in mind, the smallest-leaved kinds will be best. *Hosta lancifolia,* with long-stalked leaves about two inches wide, is one of them. It has pale lilac flowers which come in loose racemes during August and September. If the bigger-leaved species are used, a single specimen will be enough. I regard *H. sieboldiana* as the most handsome. It has large heart-shaped leaves (fourteen inches long by ten inches wide — in rich moist soils) glaucous on both sides, and pale lilac, funnel-shaped pendulous flowers carried on stems two feet long, which stand up well from the foliage. The stems should be cut right back as soon as the flowers fade.

Other species of these fine foliage plants are described in the chapter on water-gardens (*page 64*).

As regards cultivation: they really need a deep rich loam and seem to do best in partial shade, although *H. plantaginea grandiflora,* whose flowers come in October and smell of oranges, is a more successful bloomer when it is planted where the sun can get to it during some part of the day.

I have found, too, that *H. sieboldiana* thrives gloriously in quite thin sandy soils and in sunny places, provided it has a rich loam to start off with. Hostas do not need disturbing when they are established in soil that suits them. (I have an enormous clump of the above species which has not been touched for twenty years.) They are best propagated by root-division.

On each side of the stepping-stone nearest to the pool, plant a Box shrub (*Buxus sempervirens* or the smaller-leaved *B. microphylla*) or a Yew (*Taxus baccata*) clipped down low to form neat mounds. These provide a delightful contrast with the free, spreading leaves of the Hosta on the edge of the pool. Specially shaped (topiary) Box or Yew plants can be bought from most nurseries, but they are expensive; it is not difficult to shape the shrubs oneself, though it takes some years for them to become sizeable. On the other hand, clumps of the Blue Grass, *Festuca ovina glauca,* can be used; these must be left to grow freely and will provide an equally good contrast to the Hostas. This Festuca makes neat tufts of grass about six inches high and has a charming glaucous-blue colour all through the year. It doesn't lie down during the winter; and enough of it will give a permanent touch of blue to the foliage garden. In the summer, creamy grasses nine inches or so tall spring up and remain till they seed. These grasses are less attractive than the blue tufts of foliage, but it is not easy to cut them off without snipping the rest of the plant.

Festuca is easy to grow; it requires a well-dug soil containing plenty of sifted leaf mould and is completely hardy. I leave the clumps in my garden undisturbed for several years, then I divide them up; an extraordinary number of new plants can be produced from an old clump. Some gardeners part their clumps every second year, and set the new plants thus made close together to form a blue undergrowth to tall perennials. (It makes a beautiful drift of blue to Lilies.) Partial shade suits it best.

Not much stone-work will be required in a small foliage garden; but I like to have several grey flat-topped ones a few feet from the edge of the pool, facing the Hostas. (The grass should extend round the pool as a pathway.) On the north side of one of the rocks, in moist soil, plant the carpeting, creeping *Helxine soleirolii* — it is commonly known as 'Hundreds and Thousands'. It is a cress-like, bright evergreen creeper which

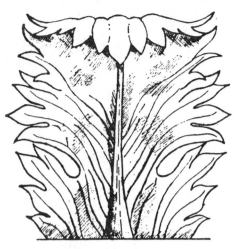

Fig. 1. The Acanthus leaf in ornamental detail from an architectural column.

Fig. 2. The Acanthus leaf that was thought to have inspired the ancient Greeks.

Fig. 3. The foliage garden: A. Pool. B. Broad-leaved Hostas. C. Clipped Box or Yew bushes. D. Blocks of stone sunk in grass. E. Hostas or Bergenias. F. Festuca or some other ornamental grass. G. Grass walk. H. Sword-shaped leaves of Iris.

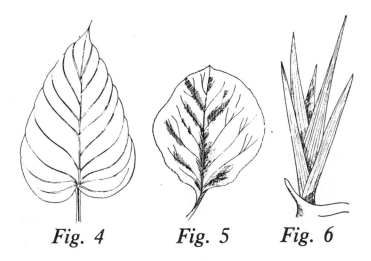

Fig. 4   Fig. 5   Fig. 6

Fig. 4. Broad leaf of the Hosta.
Fig. 5. Leaf of Bergenia ligulata: a broad,
roundish leaf.
Fig. 6. Sword-shaped leaf: Iris Germanica (our
common Purple Iris).

Fig. 7.   *Fig. 8.*
Grassy leaves.   *Fern leaf.*

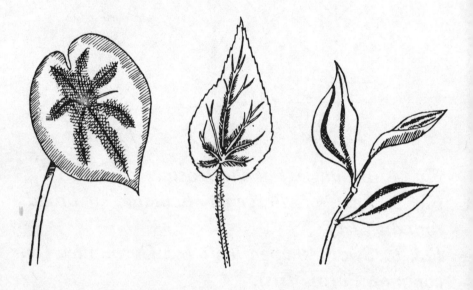

Fig. 9. Various types of patterned or variegated leaves.

covers shady damp places rapidly; but it refuses to grow in sun and is sometimes blackened by frosts. The beauty of these spreading mat-like plants is that they follow the contours of the objects on which they grow: they bulge out and they sink down with the shape of the rock.

Stones may be wholly covered with this plant, although a more artistic effect is achieved when some of the grey weathered surface is left bare.

For rocks and stones that get a lot of sun on them, an equally charming evergreen creeper can be used, viz. the fragrant, fuzzy Thyme called *Thymus pseudolanuginosus*. This plant is quite at home in full sun and once established spreads very quickly. Plant it, however, on the north side of a rock, in light leafy soil and then let it alone. It hates any sort of disturbance.

Both these foliage-creepers may be grown on a good-sized rock and will provide a contrast and a harmony of greens — the juicy green of the *Helxine* and the dry, woolly, grey-green of the *Thymus*. They are attractive, too, during the winter months.

Behind the creeper-covered rocks, I suggest planting some more Hostas; they can be the same small-leaved species planted by the edge of the pool or the charming variegated version of it, viz. *Hosta lancifolia albo-marginata* whose leaves are edged with silver-white. They should be planted in an isolated group at the bottom of the sloping bank. If something with a leaf of a different shape is preferred, plant a group of the round-leaved *Bergenia ligulata*; its dark coppery green leaves are attractive all through the year; and its pink flower-spikes come early in spring and often after a mild winter as early as February.

The sloping bank can be grassed or covered with a low-growing evergreen. The "Creeping Juniper" (*Juniperus horizontalis*) is the one that appeals to me most. It is a prostrate shrub which will cover a wide area; its dense foliage turns bright violet during the winter. The variety Douglasii, known as the Waukegan Juniper, has glaucous-blue foliage, which turns a lovely shade of purple.

These plants will probably be enough for a small foliage garden. Only half the number I suggested (twelve) are mentioned. For a large garden no doubt many more will be needed. Yet the most beautiful foliage gardens I know are those in which comparatively few different kinds are used. A large piece of ground gives us more scope; on the other hand a wide variety of plants is more difficult to dispose artistically. Over-crowding must be avoided at all costs.

If we are fortunate enough to have a natural pool or a stream, we usually want to plan a water-garden, which is quite different from a foliage garden. For many vividly coloured flowers, like the Primulas, are essentially moisture-loving plants. The water is the main feature: in the foliage garden it is merely an adjunct. And the circular pool is aesthetically more pleasing, I consider, than irregular or square shapes.

There would be room in a big foliage garden for a clump of the yellow-stemmed Bamboo *Phyllostachys aurea,* which goes up to a height of ten feet or more. Its narrow leaves are glaucous underneath. This is a good plant to choose, for it does not spread and run wildly as do so many of the Bamboos. Planted on the edge of a small pool, however, it has an odd, top-heavy look — in good rich soil it may go up to a height of fifteen feet. It shows up well set behind a bold clump of Hostas; and the largest-leaved species *Hosta sieboldiana* is the most suitable.

More rock and flag-stones can be used in the large foliage garden and will provide a perfect background for many plants. Two vertical rocks placed not too far apart make an excellent setting for the sword-like leaves of the Irises.

Iris pallida dalmatica is very beautiful in leaf; and the variegated forms of the species, one with cream-coloured stripes, the other with yellow, are among the most striking of the sword-leaf plants. The type retains its exquisite glaucous colouring till late autumn. Its flowers are lavender-blue and come in early summer.

Another good foliage Iris is the native *I. foetidissima variegata* (it can be seen in the foliage borders at University Botanic Garden, Oxford). Its narrow leaves are striped with white and lovely in the spring before the flowers appear.

These Irises have probably the most handsome leaves in the genus. They are about two feet long and show up best against grey rocks set well down in grass. The grass must be allowed to grow up close to, but not cover, the root-stocks. In the foliage garden there must be no suggestion of beds or borders. The soil must be deeply dug; and for the above-named Irises use one part each of loam, leaf mould and coarse sand.

It is said that the Japanese grow only evergreens in their foliage gardens; they dislike the bare branches of deciduous shrubs and trees in winter. Evergreens should certainly predominate, but I should like to include one of the beautiful, deciduous Japanese Maples. The brilliant red-leaved forms are too conspicuous, however, among the prevailing tones of green. *Acer palmatum dissectum*, with finely cut bright green leaves, is the Maple to choose. It is a dwarf mushroom-shaped shrub in its young state and, as it matures, grows rounded and makes a wonderful specimen plant. When it is fully grown, it will be the 'show-plant' in the garden, therefore it needs careful placing. Set it in the background — it would look wonderful on a grass-covered slope. It is not tender, as some gardeners imagine it to be, but its delicate foliage is often nipped by late spring frosts; so it should be given some protection when a cold spell is imminent. As it grows older, it seems to become less susceptible to frost damage. It wants a rich moist soil, rather on the acid side: equal parts of sifted peat or leaf mould and sandy loam make an excellent medium for it. The ground must be perfectly drained.

This Japanese Maple, when it changes colour in the autumn, will probably be the most striking of all the plants I have mentioned. In a foliage garden colour takes a secondary place; in fact, it scarcely enters into the planting scheme. It is possible to achieve some unusual effects with the silver-leaved plants. *Senecio greyii* (*S. laxifolius*), with its white-felted foliage, set against a closely clipped Yew hedge shows up in a remarkable way; the two together producing a curiously beautiful effect of black and white.

The leaves of these foliage plants provide us with a wide variety of shapes; some, as in *Iris foetidissima*, are truly evergreen and very pleasing to see during the winter.

I was once asked whether a tall Cactus form like *Leptocereus schottii* could be used in a foliage garden; it is an exotic from North-west Mexico and would have to be left in its pot. It seems out of place to me. It is a slender, ridged, spiny succulent, perhaps in its younger state four feet tall. A garden designer suggested that it could be stood in its pot on a flag-stone near the edge of a pool and would look less incongruous there than anywhere else, especially if a clump of Bamboos were in the vicinity.

CHAPTER II

Foliage Plants in the Herbaceous Border

PROBABLY the first serious attempt to employ foliage plants decoratively in our gardens was in the herbaceous border, which reached the height of its popularity about the beginning of the century. The long, wide border, in which only flowers are used, is common enough. And coming across one a blaze of colour is a little startling. There is too much to take in. This is especialy felt, when little thought has been given to the planning. But some sort of scheme can be observed in most of them, even if it only boils down to the tallest plants at the back and the shortest in the front. There are better ways of planning the all-flower border: the palest colours should be set at the ends and by gradation lead up to the most vivid ones in the centre, so the eye moves slowly along from soft pastel shades to the most intense scarlets or blues. If this method is used, there will be no hard clashes of colour.

The finest effects are obtained, however, by the judicious use of foliage plants, especially those with glaucous-green, grey-green and silvery grey leaves. The Hosta is one of the most valuable. It is useful for providing contrast and toning-down too vivid colour effects. Its cool-looking broad leaves soften the hard scarlet of *Lobelia cardinalis* and enhance the beauty of the bright velvety blue *Salvia patens*.

One specimen of the large-leaved species *Hosta sieboldiana* is enough for interposing between clumps of vividly coloured flowers. It is a good choice because its leaves are unpatterned.

A smaller-leaved kind like *H. lancifolia* is very desirable as an edging and in a long border can be grouped to extend some six feet in length. The variety *albo-marginata*, with white-margined leaves, is very effective. On the other hand, these smaller kinds can be massed in big clumps (in large borders, of course) to form a sort of bay which extends a few feet back into the border.

Variegated foliage plants, with their coloured stripes or blotches, are most decorative and blend well with flowers. One of the finest is *Tulipa greigii*; it is an early spring-blooming Tulip species with cup-shaped, bright scarlet flowers; but its foliage is as beautiful in its way as the flowers. The broad, pointed leaves, eight inches long and about four inches wide, are rather like those of a small Hosta. They are very glaucous, the bluish grey upper surface being marked with reddish purple specks in longitudinal lines. The flowers are removed as soon as they fade; and for many weeks the leaves retain their charming colouring. They make smallish round clumps and are ideal for edging part of the border. The plant flourishes in ordinary soil and revels in full sun.

Although I have seen the dwarf variegated grass *Arrhenatherum elatius bulbosum variegatum* used in the front of many borders, I don't recommend it for a small one as it is such a wild spreader. It soon makes large clumps and works its way insidiously among the closely set stems of many perennials. But it is bright and attractive and good to see during the winter. It can be controlled by planting it in a shallow tub about eighteen inches wide, which should be sunk well down in the soil. This will prevent the plant from spreading. Another method is to sink corrugated iron round the plant; the intervening space between it and the edge of the iron can be filled with annuals or biennials, which are lifted after they have flowered. This ornamental grass has whitish stripes, the white and green colouring looking particularly attractive associated with the blue-grey foliage of the hardy Pinks.

The Festuca (the popular Blue Grass) is not invasive — it makes big clumps in time — and can be planted anywhere in the front or the middle row of the border. If groups of the hardy Lily *Lilium regale* are grown, use it as a ground-work; the drift of blue among the tall-stemmed Lilies (white stained with reddish purple) is a delightful association. A lovely effect is obtained when it is used similarly with the tangerine-orange Lily *L. bulbiferum croseum* (*L. croceum*), the old-fashioned Orange Lily with erect flowers. Both Lilies must be planted well toward the front so that the blue grass is clearly visible.

The variegated Aubrietia *Aubrietia deltoida variegata*, with small green-and-yellow leaves (some wholly yellow), is occasionally used as an edging in an herbaceous border. It is perhaps more suitable in a rockery, where it has a better chance to display its pretty foliage.

Dwarf plants, six inches or so high, are mostly planted in the front row; this is necessary in a small border. A long edging of dwarf plants of uniform height tends to monotony, however; and in a long border a few clumps of taller plants should be introduced to give variety.

Salvia officinalis purpurescens, the purplish variety of the common culinary herb, appears to be quite rare in many districts. It is not above eighteen inches tall but with its pink-purple woolly leaves makes a conspicuous break of warm colour in the front row. This plant grows well in ordinary garden soil; it spreads out into a large clump and may need dividing up after a few years. Practically any colour goes well with it. The old-fashioned Scarlet Geraniums (Zonal Pelargoniums) look even more scarlet when grown beside it; so does the scarlet Lobelia already referred to.

The silver-leaved Lavender Cotton (*Santolina chamaecyparissus*) is probably the best known and the most frequently seen of the foliage plants we grow in this country. It is at its loveliest when its young leaves begin to turn from grey-green to silvery white; and it is least attractive when covered with its hard yellow flower-heads. Most gardeners cut them off.

It does best in thin sandy soils. It doesn't like

rich loams and will not live long in badly drained ground. The sandier the soil, the whiter the foliage. This should be remembered when planting the shrub in the herbaceous border, where the soil is consistently rich. A hole at the edge should be made for it; fill it with rubble and poor sandy soil; the plant will thrive in that.

After a year or two the plant begins to lose its shape and becomes spreading and lax; pruning it back hard in late autumn will help to keep it bushy. But I prefer to take cuttings every summer; they root quickly out of doors and should be planted out in a double row about March. These are far more effective as an edging than a flopping, mature shrub. (In formal beds it is often used for a silver-white edging; the young plants are neatly clipped, sides and top, and shape up well.) The dwarf variety *nana* is better for a small border and charming in the rockery. Both are excellent for toning down vivid colours and for setting between clumps of flowers whose colours clash.

Artemisia abrotanum, the Southernwood, is equally popular (both it and the Lavender Cotton were in cultivation here during the sixteenth century) and, like that plant, thrives in poor sandy soil. It is deciduous and therefore of no ornamental value during the winter — the Santolinas are evergreen. Its fine, feathery green foliage is strongly aromatic after rain and very pleasant. The plant attains a height of about four feet and makes a nicely shaped erect slender bush of much neater habit than the Lavender Cotton.

It is a good foliage plant to set by a group of border Phloxes (*Phlox paniculata*), the soft foliage contrasting ideally with the heavy flower-heads, purple, pink, scarlet, violet-blue, etc.

The white downy-leaved *Artemisia palmeri* is not so well known. It is very striking in a clump and harmonises beautifully with pale colours such as lavender and pink. Placed toward the front of the border, it makes a pleasing cool break in a row of flowers.

The Hosta, the Lavender Cotton and this particular Artemisia may be grouped to form a charming centre-piece for a border; or they can be associated with certain flowers to form an imposing isolated group. A photograph published in *Country Life* some years ago showed this magnificent association in a Surrey garden. Young plants of the silver Santolina were set in a row eighteen inches long between a large specimen of *Hosta sieboldiana* on the left, and *Artemisia palmeri* massed in a clump on the right. These three different types of foliage plants contrasted perfectly with one another; the broad, cool green leaves of the Hosta spreading out on to the path, the curly silver-white Santolina plants in a row and the tall, loose clump of white downy Artemisia close to them.

Immediately behind the Santolina was a dwarf white Hydrangea, about eighteen inches high. (I imagine it was a one-year-old plant of the lovely, pure white 'Mme. E. Mouillère'.) In the next row were the slender graceful stems of *Salvia* × *superba* (*S. virgata nemorosa*) covered with purple flowers. These contrasted strikingly with the rounded white heads of the Hydrangea. And behind the Salvia was a tall clump of pale pink Sweet Peas growing freely up Beech twigs. Again a charming contrast in colour and form.

A closely clipped black-green Yew hedge about six feet tall provided the perfect background. Such a striking group as this should be used as a centre-piece or motif in a small, narrow border.

Of the vividly coloured foliage plants, every

man to his own choice. For my part, I don't care to see many of them used in conjunction with our ordinary herbaceous-border flowers. The coppery red leaf of the common Beetroot is one of the least showy. It looks best near bright reds or blues. The fresh, shining green leaves of the Spinach give us a cool patch of colour: the plant should be grouped in a bold clump in the front row. (Like the Beetroot, it needs a well-worked rich soil).

Scrophularia nodosa variegata (the common Figwort) is a perennial about two feet tall, with dark green ovalish leaves variegated with yellow creamy markings. Its flowers are insignificant. A useful foliage plant for growing in a clump and for interposing between groups of vividly coloured flowers.

A plant that can be similarly used is *Euphorbia characias*, a bushy plant six feet tall, with narrow bluish green leaves up the stems, which terminate in a long inflorescence composed of round greenish yellow flowers or bracts standing out conspicuously on long stalks. It is something of a giant, rather ungainly looking and suitable only for large borders. The outer stems flop and may need supporting. Grow it with tall, robust

Delphiniums like the mauve-blue 'Cambria' or the six-foot 'Valentia', which has deep blue flowers. I have seen it, too, massed behind large clumps of the pure white Madonna Lily (*Lilium candidum*).

Thalictrum speciosissimum has very glaucous foliage (shaped like that of a giant Maindenhair-fern) which is an excellent foil to the Madonna Lily and the Delphinium. It is a fairly common border perennial, about five feet tall and has small heads of pale yellow, fluffy flowers — of less value in the border than the leaves.

The famous *Acanthus spinosus* is another perennial which is prized for its foliage. I grow it in the front row, next to a clump of *Hosta sieboldiana*, whose smooth glaucous-green leaves contrast well with the spiny, deeply divided leaves (dark green) of the Acanthus. The flowers are cut off as soon as they fade. The plant does well in shade — which suits the Hosta.

There is a fine foliage Honesty called *Lunaria annua variegata*, whose flowers are of a bluish violet colour and much more attractive than the hard magenta-coloured ones of the common type plant. The leaves are almost wholly cream and white: they are so different from those of the common Honesty that one doesn't associate the variegated plant with it. The small leaves or bracts on the inflorescence stem are almost a pure white. This Honesty is in full bloom in late April, before the main show of the border begins. Actually, it is difficult to find a suitable flowering plant to associate with it. I grow it in a clump (it attains about two feet in height) toward the front of the border and have Oriental Poppies (*Papaver orientale* — three to four feet tall) behind. They do not bloom till May or June, but their thick green divided leaves provide a good contrasting background to the cream and white of the Honesty. The flowers of this plant do not last long, but the foliage is attractive all through the summer and harmonises well with the less vividly coloured flowers of the Oriental Poppies such as the double, pink 'Salmon Glow'.

Stachys lanata is a white, woolly leaved perennial (Lamb's Tongue), well known in our gardens. Its flowers, small and bright purple, come in a branched spike; it is a hard colour which is not greatly liked by most people. But the soft thick leaves have an artificial look about them which is uncommonly beautiful. Gardeners who like to have their plants in rows in a border, should use this Stachys along with the Cotton Lavender and *Senecio cineraria* (the Dusty Miller). Set the plants close enough together to form an unbroken line — as the Cotton Lavender is the largest, fewer specimens of it will be required. This "silver line" is most effective woven through the middle of the herbaceous border.

Senecio cineraria is seldom above eighteen inches tall and can be kept smaller by pinching out the top. The deeply lobed leaves, two to six inches long, are of a grey-white felt-like texture, the stems white and furry. It is often used in formal beds where it is particularly useful for toning down such vividly coloured plants as *Begonia rex* and its varieties.

CHAPTER III

The Rockery

FOLIAGE plants are especially valuable in the rockery, since most alpines bloom in early spring and are past their best by May. From May onwards this feature, in small gardens particularly, is often something of an eyesore with its mounds of fading Aubretia, Arabis and Alyssum. Yet there is a wide choice of suitable alpine or semi-alpine foliage plants to make it attractive all through the year. Few gardeners seem to use them, however.

The ideal rockery, of course, is the one constructed of good natural rock or stone on a site that is a little below the level of the ground. For most alpines are moisture-loving plants and in this position, given the soil they need, will never suffer from drought. Too often, unfortunately, the average rockery we see is not much more than a pile of rocks embedded in soil several feet high above the surface. This may be all right for certain creepers and spreading succulents that don't mind desert-like conditions. (Aubretia, Arabis and Alyssum grow well in dry walls but give a better display and last longer in flower in low well-drained ground.)

The slope or sunk ground in which the rocks are embedded is mostly grassed, and if this is kept clipped low it is pleasant to see and shows up the rocks to best advantage.

But there is the Alpine Lawn which, although lacking the fresh green of the grass, provides us with a delightful blend of grey and green carpeting plants.

One of the best of these is the Thyme already mentioned, viz. *Thymus pseudolanuginosus*. It spreads quickly once established in a light leafy sandy loam and becomes a pretty mat of grey woolly leaves covered with a silky down. When you tread gently on the plant, it gives off its warm pungent smell.

The creeping Thyme of our hedgerows and fields is *Thymus serpyllum*, a strong, hardy plant that gets a lot of treading on in the wild. There are numerous garden forms of it, but none is so lovely, I think, as the grey woolly species just mentioned. From the Clarence Elliot Nurseries

I have in the past had *T. serpyllum* 'Cloth of Gold', which is a sunny yellow in summer and green all through the winter; *albus*, covered with white flowers during the summer; and the strongly fragrant 'Nosegay'. These few carpeting Thymes will soon cover a good-sized piece of ground.

A fine plant to mix with them is the white winter Heather *Erica carnea alba*, a vigorous, spreading mat-plant said to be as tough as grass — so an excellent choice for the Alpine Lawn. Its foliage, a bright yellow-green in spring and summer, turns a darker colour at the end of the year. It does best in a leafy, rather acid soil. The Thymes, on the other hand, need a light sandy loam.. All these plants are good to look at and suffer no harm from being trodden on. There are other carpeters equally suitable for the Alpine Lawn: the *Acaena* and the *Antennaria* genera, for example, supply us with some very attractive kinds. But many are more valuable in the rockery, partly covering the rocks (like the evergreen cress *Helxine soleirolii*) or standing up conspicuously in front of, or near, fading alpines.

Artemisia armeniaca (native of Armenia) is one of the best for rock-work. Elliott's catalogue describes it as *A. canescens*: "An exceedingly

41

beautiful sub-shrub for rock gardens, wall garden or border. Erect, graceful branches, which are a cloud of silver filigree foliage." It has stems about eighteen inches long and narrow leaves covered with silver-white down; it grows well in any ordinary soil.

Another species about the same size is *A. frigida*, which makes a shrubby ground cover in the wild. (In parts of North America it is commonly known as the "Mountain Fringe".) Its foliage is finely divided into silver silky lobes and retains its colour better when it is clipped over in early spring.

A charming silver-green carpeter is the New Zealand *Acaena buchananii*. It can be used for covering a flat-topped rock against which Aubrietia or Arabis is growing; the flowers of these plants should be cut off as soon as they have faded.

Acaena microphylla is another: an evergreen mat-forming plant (about two inches high), which spreads rapidly; its foliage is a greyish bronze colour, and the small flowers are red and spiny. Both species are choice foliage plants and useful for growing near flowering alpines which fade quickly. These Acaenas thrive in either damp or dry places.

The Achilleas, on the other hand, like well-drained sunny places. *Achillea clavenae* will flourish in sand and is prized for its silver leaves. It grows about six inches tall and makes a tufted hoary plant with white flowers in summer. I like to see it massed in a pocket, with a grey rock behind it. The plant is described in Vol. 31 of the *Botanical Magazine* (1810). It was apparently first discovered in the Alps of Austria and Stiria by Clusius, where it grew "in the crevices of the rocks and frightful precipices. . . . The *Achillea clavenae* may be considered as a connecting link between this genus and *Artemisia*. . . . Cultivated by Mr. James Sutherland, in the Edinburgh Botanic Garden, in the year 1683".

Some of the Cudweeds or Everlastings are excellent mat-forming plants. *Antennaria dioica minima*, an inch tall, is one of the best and a favourite of mine. The plant is sometimes used in Alpine Lawns, where it provides a drift of minute pink flowers for a few weeks in May; but its great charm is its silver-grey foliage. This alpine is especially suitable for growing in miniature "sink-gardens"; in the rockery it should be allowed to cover the surface of a flat slab of grey stone.

A. dioica tomentosum, which has white flowers four to five inches high, is a stronger grower than the other; its leaves are downy and show up their soft colouring best on a paved walk. Plant it in the interstices of a stone pathway which leads through the rock-garden.

One of the most delightful of all carpeting alpines is the evergreen *Arenaria balearica*. It can only be grown, however, in shady moist places; it will not live in dry sunny rock-gardens. The finest specimens I have seen were those growing near water, where the plants were set in cool moist soil next to a flat-topped rock used as an edging to a pool. The base of the rock was submerged, the water keeping the surrounding soil consistently moist.

This Arenaria spreads rapidly in such places, covering the rocks or the ground with mats of emerald-green — rather like moss. The flowers, white and minute, come on tiny stalks and are pin's-head-sized.

In many districts the plant retains its fresh green colour all through the winter; occasionally, however, like *Helxine soleirolii* (the Creeping Cress) it is blackened by frost. If these two are grown together, they should be given plenty of room and kept well away from any choice creeper, for they will soon smother it. I have seen the Arenaria overrun with the other plant.

Several species of *Armeria* are grown in our gardens. They are the Thrifts or Sea Pinks, useful for an edging, with their neat evergreen tufts, and massed in the rockery they give us a pleasing show of foliage through the winter. *Armeria montana*, about three inches high, is one of the dwarfest: a dainty little alpine for grouping close against a rock. The variety *rubra* is more dwarf in habit, its red flowers coming on stalks only an inch high. It blooms in May.

One of the best for a show of coloured foliage in autumn and winter is *A. maritima variegata*; it makes an attractive drift of golden-yellow (the tufts are from six to twelve inches high) for hiding faded clumps of spring-blooming alpines.

The variegated Aubrietias are valuable for the mats of coloured leaves they provide; *Aubrietias deltoidea aurea variegata* is quite brilliant through the winter months. It flourishes luxuriantly in light sandy soil and likes a sunny position.

Aubrietia, Arabis and *Alyssum* are probably the commonest alpines in our gardens and there are variegated forms of them obtainable from most nurseries. Although many gardeners do not care for variegated foliage, the yellow markings on the leaves of these plants give us some bright patches of colour when the flowers are past. *Alyssum saxatile variegatum* (yellow and grey-green) is delightful on top of a rockery-wall. It is less frequently seen than the variegated Arabis *Arabis albida variegata*, whose leaves are blotched with yellow; this is the single-flowered plant; the double form is *A. albida flore pleno variegata*. Both are valuable mat-forming plants for the winter.

The leaves of the hardy Cyclamen *Cyclamen neapolitanum* (roughly Ivy-shaped) are totally different from those of the alpines we have considered. The variegations give a beautiful marbled effect to the leaves. They come after the flowers (which bloom in autumn) and persist till the spring. Give the plants a shady spot in well-drained leafy loam and never disturb them. The corms should be covered with gritty soil. This hardy Cyclamen (it has pink flowers) usually seeds freely and in time will make a very charming ground cover.

Dianthus (Pinks) are much admired for their

46

blue-grey foliage; the old-fashioned 'Mrs. Sinkins' is one of the most popular — its foliage gives a sharp grey edging to any border. *Dianthus gratianopolitanus* (*D. caesius*), the Cheddar Pink, is by far the best known of the alpine species (it is a native of Britain) and easily accommodated in the average rockery. It is mostly used as a trailer: planted on the top of a low rock-wall or a retaining-wall and allowed to ramble at will. In too rich a soil it is said to be a poor bloomer; but I have found that it refuses to bloom at all in thin soils that dry out completely during the summer. The foliage, however, retains its exquisite glaucous-blue colouring; and this is particularly valuable during the winter. Although the flowers do not last long, they are some of the most fragrant we grow and it is worth giving the plant the soil it likes in order to get them. A light gritty soil containing a little sifted leaf mould is the best medium to start it off in.

Much dwarfer is *D. alpinus*, four inches high (about half the height of the Cheddar Pink), its tufted foliage being grass-green and making fresh patches of colour before the flowers appear.

If I were limited in my choice to only one foliage plant for the rockery, I should want

Sedum spathulifolium purpureum, which Clarence Elliot calls the finest Sedum in cultivation — "leaves plum purple with a grey bloom". They come in rosettes, are typically succulent and only lose their juicy look when the plants are grown in starved dry soils. The leaves then become deep red and are much smaller. But in ordinary sandy loam, which the plant likes, they are an enchanting glaucous-plum-purple colour. The rosettes spread out and in time form a carpeting mass as beautiful as that made by the marbled leaves of *Cyclamen neapolitanum*. The Sedum flowers are bright yellow and are carried on three-inch stalks in May. I do not care for them and cut them off.

The plant spreads by means of its runner-like base stems, which carry the new leaf-rosettes, these being green and mealy at first. I can think of nothing quite so lovely for the winter than a wide patch of it growing along the ground or patches of it on a vertical rock.

It will grow practically anywhere, though its appearance is influenced markedly by soil and situation. I start it off in a mixture of two parts of coarse sand and one part each of leaf mould and loam. It likes full sun and in shade loses most of its exquisite colouring. It is easily propagated by pulling off some of the side shoots, which have roots attached, and planting the pieces firmly in sandy soil. In my garden I have often come across bits of the plant dropped in odd places by birds. They seem specially attracted by it when it is growing in the crevices of a wall. The plant usually roots wherever it falls.

The Stonecrop (*Sedum acre*), with tiny pulpy leaves, is the best known of all the Sedums and grows on brick walls, roofs and in places where few other plants can exist. It is the most invasive of all rock-plants; I pull up handfuls of it to keep it from smothering other more valuable things.

There is a variegated form called *aureum* whose leaves are a bright golden-yellow in the spring. Unfortunately it loses its bright colour after May. Neither plant by the way is suitable for the Alpine Lawn.

The Cobweb Houseleek (*Sempervivum arachnoideum*), another well-known succulent, is often grown in a pot — probably because it is thought to be rather tender. It is a dry-looking, hairy plant, the antithesis of the juicy *Sedum apathulifolium purpureum*.

The tips of the leaves forming the rosettes of

the Cobwebb Houseleek are connected by fine soft white hairs, which give the plant its singular charm. I grow it on a ledge on a low rock-wall, where it has made a smallish patch of grey-green colour. One or two flower-spikes shoot out in midsummer. They come on stems three to four inches long; the individual flowers, pink, are star-shaped and about one inch across.

The plant needs the minimum amount of soil but should be started off in a medium rich in humus; it will then go ahead. It spreads rather slowly, the young rosettes forming round the parent plant. This succulent and the other two preceding ones when grown together give us an exquisite patch of opalescent colour — but a watch must be kept on the Stonecrop (*Sedum acre*).

Grass-shaped leaves are provided by the Thrifts (*Armeria*) described on *page 45* ; the popular Blue Grass (*Festuca*) can also be used, planted in drifts against the rocks or set in a clump higher up on a rocky ledge.

An uncommon ornamental grass is the variegated *Acorus gramineus variegatus*, whose leaves (about an eighth of an inch wide) are striped with white and are eight inches long. It likes a moist soil and is often planted near water or actually in water. I have grown it at the base of a boulder where it formed pleasing grassy tufts in a very short time.

For dwarf, sword-shaped leaves, use the tiny Irises like *Iris pumila*. It is six inches high, the purple-blue forms resembling in miniature our common Flag-iris *I. germanica*. As a pocket plant, wholly or partly surrounded by rock-work it is admirable. It is an excellent place in which to grow it, the rocks keeping the spreading underground stems from encroaching on any other parts of the rockery.

There are numerous garden forms: var. *lutea*, yellow; var. *attica*, pale yellow flowers tinged with green and marked with brownish spots; var. *azurea* has pale blue flowers and is one of the loveliest of the tribe. These Irises make dense, rapidly spreading clumps and flower best in a well-drained gritty loam containing plenty of humus. I have succeeded in growing them in quite narrow crevices where they get the minimum amount of nutriment; they cannot spread in such a position and they scarcely produce any flowers. The blooming season is very short.

I. cristata is another dwarf Iris which spreads

by means of its creeping root stems or rhizomes. Its leaves are about four inches high, its flowers a pale blue with a yellow crest.

Even smaller is *I. lacustris* with narrow leaves which are sometimes wavy margined. Its flowers are a pretty shade of pale violet. As soon as the flowers fade, nip them off; the foliage, with which we are most concerned, then shows up to best advantage.

For broad-leaved plants to provide contrast, there is *Hosta lancifolia tardiflora*, which has leaves five inches long and two inches wide, and when in flower, during September, seldom grows more than ten inches high. There is only one place for it, and that is at the foot of a cool grey boulder. This is the most suitable of the species for limited spaces.

For the large rockery any of them may be used, the variegated kinds like *H. fortunei marginata-alba* (white-margined leaves) looking particularly handsome against grey rock-work.

Vividly coloured foliage plants are out of place among the rocks (more so here perhaps than anywhere); nonetheless I have seen that delightful Saxifrage known as "Mother of Thousands" growing on the shady, sheltered side of a boulder.

It is offered by most nurseries under the name of *Saxifraga sarmentosa* but is usually described now as *S. stolonifera*; it has round, richly veined or marbled leaves on long stalks, and sends out running stems or stolons bearing the new plants. The flowers, white and yellow, come on stalks nine inches tall but are not very striking. The foliage is most ornamental; and the plant will survive cold weather if it is grown in poor soil and given some protection. It is often sold as a pot-plant; and it is, I think, one of the most suitable for the formal bed.

There are of course many other foliage plants which we can grow in our rockeries and some of these are included in the descriptive list at the end of the book. Their chief purpose, as in the herbaceous border, is to provide variety and contrast, and many of them serve a double purpose when they help to hide the faded flowers of alpines that have bloomed early in the year.

CHAPTER IV

Formal Beds

MOST gardeners like to try their hand at Carpet-bedding. It needs skill and patience and entails plenty of work, especially if an elaborate design is attempted. For this type of formal bed, foliage plants, usually the low-growing compact kind are mostly used. Carpet-bedding was very popular with the Victorians and no doubt the idea was to imitate the designs in the colourful carpets imported from the East.

These beds are much less popular with amateurs nowadays and are seen usually in parks and public gardens where the planting-out is done by skilled gardeners.

Many of the plants are tender or partly tender and are not put out till June, when the danger of frost is past. Designs are numerous (there are standard ones); but the tendency today is towards simplification; I say this, comparing those I see (quite rarely now in gardens) with those of the past.

The soil should be loamy and contain plenty of sifted leaf mould or some moisture-retaining composts. It must be made firm to receive the plants. (Tread it down gently on a fine sunny morning and do the planting in the evening.) The lines of the design are drawn with the end of a trowel, and these are then traced with white sand to guide the planter.

What sort of foliage plants do the professionals use to get their wonderful effects? You can see a good choice at Kew: on the lawn in front of the Palm-house they are set out in segregated groups — to exhibit them — but not in the flowing lines of any intricate design. And nearby is a large round bed planted with a variety of egregious Cacti and succulents. Tall, spiny, ridged plants, some more like solid sticks of carved wax than living plants. But the flat rosette succulents, such as the *Echeveria*, are the ones that are used for Carpet-bedding.

Of course these are not plants that have to be clipped. Many are grown in small pots, four or six inches across, each pot containing a single rosette. At Kew in June *Echeveria potosina* (from the Southern U.S.A.) is about six inches across and has tall, mealy, untidy flower-spikes. These flowers must be cut off, for they detract from the appearance of the closely set lines of the design. The rosette is an exquisite white-blue colour and of a wax-like texture.

Another growing in the same bed at Kew and as lovely as this plant is *E. simulans*. They are about the same size. The latter is glaucous-green; the fleshy leaves are also waxen-looking but tipped with pink. Both are ideal for filling in a circle in the centre of a round bed. Or, where there is a good stock of them, they can be used for edging a large bed, the rosettes being set out so that they almost touch one another.

E. glauca is well known and forms rosettes about four inches across, the rounded leaves being blue-grey with reddish margins.

As Echeverias like a sandy soil, it is advisable to add a little to the soil when they are planted.

They are readily increased by offsets or by detaching the fleshy leaves, which will root quickly in sand.

In late autumn the plants must be lifted and housed in a temperature of about 40°F. Most of the species are natives of Mexico, Texas and California, where they get all the sun they need.

The *Iresine* is a half-hardy foliage perennial and may be seen at Kew exhibited in groups in a formal bed, by the Palm-house. The leaves, heart-shaped or lanceolate, are different shades of red, green or gold. My own favourite is *Iresine lindenii*, which has blackish Beetroot-coloured leaves and in early summer is about six inches high. The upper leaves, lanceolate, are about two inches long; the plants should be set four to six inches apart so that the leaves touch and give a thick dense line or a dense patch of colour.

I. × *brilliantissima* may also be seen at Kew (it is usually listed as *I. herbstii* var. *brilliantissima*); its leaves are beautifully coloured pink and carmine; the plant is about four inches high in June. These Iresines should clipped back when they begin to grow to keep them in neat lines or within the bounds of the shapes they fill. (I have kept them down to six inches by repeated clippings.) If they overspill, the design or the pattern is ruined.

The usual method when only a few are grown is simply to pinch out the tops; this makes them bushy. The flowers, white or greenish white and inconspicuous, will not form if this is done during the growing season, which is June and July.

I. herbstii var. *wallisii* is very dwarf and, if kept pinched back, makes a useful filling-in plant for the smaller details of a design. The leaves are ovalish, recurved and a startling black-purple colour.

Like the Echeverias, the Iresines come from the hotter regions of the U.S.A. and cannot be left out in our gardens through the winter. Cuttings (side shoots with a heel) should be taken and inserted in and in a frame during August. They root quickly and should then be brought inside and kept in a temperature of about 55°F. through the winter.

Echeverias and Iresines are seldom grown by amateurs; they see them frequently perhaps in the formal beds of their municipal gardens and rightly conclude that there could be no better way of using them, for they are among the most artificial-looking of plants. Beautiful many of them are, but their bizarre colourings clash badly with most of the herbaceous plants we grow.

Coleus provide some striking colours, too, and they and the Iresines are widely used in Carpet-bedding schemes. Several varieties, labelled, may be seen at Kew. *Coleus* × 'Roi de Noir' has nettle-shaped leaves, about three inches long, of

58

a deep copper-maroon colour. Another, *C.* ✕ 'Golden Ball' has yellow-gold leaves and can be kept clipped back to about four inches high — a fine plant for ribbon-planting (this is simply setting the plants out in a single line, which may run straight or curve round to form a pattern).

The garden varieties of *Coleus* used are derived ·from a hybrid of *C. blumei*, a Japanese species. The variety *C. blumei* var. *verschaffeltii* (purple-red foliage) is an old form and responsible for numerous modern kinds. My own favourites are 'Vesuvius', red leaves edged with gold; 'Diane', deep pink edged with green; and 'Mrs. Sanders', which has variegated leaves, red, green and yellow, and is a dwarf grower of dense habit.

Like the Iresines, these Coleus should be pinched back to make them more bushy; I have often lightly clipped over the red 'Vesuvius' when it has been used as a "single-line" plant. This variety and the red-leaved *vershaffeltii* are often planted next to the furry, silver-grey Lavender Cotton (*Santolina chamaecyparissus*), the latter being used as an edging to a Carpet-bedding design and closely clipped to make a surround six inches high and four inches wide.

Cuttings of these bedding Coleus can be taken

at any time of the year. They should be inserted in sand in thumb pots and allowed to root in a temperature of about 60°F. Gardeners who require large quantities usually raise their plants from seed, sowing in a temperature of 65°F. at the end of February. Deep pans containing a light sandy compost are used and the seedlings pricked out as soon as they are big enough to handle.

The strongest-growing seedlings are those with a preponderance of green in their colouring and consequently of little ornamental value. These should be removed and thrown away; the weaker ones, which invariably produce the richest colours (the purple-reds and brilliant yellows), are grown on in small pots and then planted out in the form bed about mid-June.

Echeveria, Iresine and Coleus seem to be the three most popular bedding plants in many of the public gardens I know. The long stems carrying the Echeveria flowers are always cut off; and the other two are kept neatly clipped, or, when only a few are needed, simply pinched. If this isn't done, they soon spread out and run into the other plants.

One could easily find another dozen genera

containing suitable foliage plants for the formal bed; and there are of course many with both coloured foliage and attractive flowers. The common bedder, the Geranium, or Zonal Pelargonium, is a special favourite. There is a charming little variety called 'General MacArthur', whose small round leaves are yellow margined with scarlet; it would make a striking filling-in plant for a section of a design. (The flowers are sometimes pinched out.)

The genus *Fuchsia* has a Group with ornamental leaves; the flowers, unlike those of the Geraniums, are insignificant. The one in a formal bed at Kew, labelled *Fuchsia* X 'Golden Treasure', is one of the best.

Its leaves are a bright golden-yellow, shaped rather like those of the Golden Privet. The flowers are invariably pinched, when the plant is used in Carpet-bedding. It needs full sunlight to bring out the glowing yellow colour; planted in shade its foliage turns an uninteresting green.

I have seen varieties of *Alternanthera*, *Antennaria* and *Centaurea* being planted out in formal beds by gardeners. Some have complained about the names and wished they had simple English ones. I don't know of any popular name for the *Alteranthera*. Many of the species are now described under *Telanthera*; and these are known to some gardeners as 'Joy-weeds'. Several give a bright colourful display of foliage. *T. ficoidea* (*Alternanthera amabilis*), from Tropical America, has orange-scarlet leaves and is rated high by gardeners.

Antennaria has the popular names of 'Cudweed' and Cat's-ear'; no doubt the latter refers to the soft silver-white leaves. *A. dioica tomentosum* (*see page 43*) is a favourite bedder and should have its flowers pinched out.

Centaureas are the Cornflowers, Sweet Sultans, Centaury. *C. dealbata* is the 'Mealy Centaury'; its leaves are white and downy beneath, but I have never seen it used in the formal bed. *C. ragusina* var. *compacta*, with silvery, hairy foliage is the favourite one; it averages a foot high and is of compact habit. Like many of the bedders described in this chapter, it is half-hardy and should be housed through the winter.

Cerastium tomentosum is 'Snow in Summer', a plant listed by some writers as a good bedder, but I don't recommend it: it is far too invasive and quickly smothers everything growing near it. (*See the descriptive list, page 123*).

Saxifrage stolonifera, with its small round, marbled leaves, is one of the loveliest plants for edging a formal bed; but the favourite way to grow it is to mass it in a circle in the middle of a Carpet-bedding design.

The last we shall mention is in my opinion the most striking: the king of foliage plants: *Begonia rex*, which comes from the colourful province of Assam in North-east India. This magnificent plant has produced numerous garden varieties with a wide range of very beautiful markings — some a brilliant purple, red and pink, touched here and there with silver and green. They are hardly suitable, however, for the Carpet-bed: for one thing they need shade and most of the other bedders must have full sun. They also need a rich peaty soil and ample moisture. They are ideal for filling a bed somewhere on a shady lawn. The vivid purples, pinks, and reds of the leaves provide all the colour that is necessary and the grass surround makes the perfect setting.

CHAPTER V

The Water-Garden

IT is in the water-garden that some of the handsomest foliage plants are grown. The Gunneras (like giant Rhubarbs); Rheums, which have similarly shaped leaves; tall, fifteen-foot (or more) Bamboos; the Lysichitums, known as the Bog Arums, with their huge shining spinach-green leaves, three feet long and one foot wide and lemon-yellow Arum-lily flowers; there are many others, but these I like particularly and they are, I think, the most arresting.

In some gardens in this district, thirty miles east of London, *Gunnera manicata* is covered up with Bracken during the winter to protect its new growths from late spring frosts. I first saw this done at the Savill Gardens, Windsor. But the plant is hardy enough in our southern counties.

Seeing Bracken heaped on it one April, reminded me of Rhubarb being forced by having a layer of straw put on it. It was the middle of the month, the thick fleshy stems carrying the embryo leaves had forced their way up through the dead foliage to a height of four feet. The plant is egregiously showy in its young state, quite artificial-looking with its green-yellow stems covered with short decurved red-tipped prickles; smaller ones, a deep carmine-red, come more thickly on the mid-ribs of the leaves.

There is no more suitable place for this giant foliage plant than the water-garden. It needs deep, moist, rich soil such as is to be found by the side of a stream; and with its enormous leaves, eight feet or more wide, it can be grown only in very large gardens.

In passing it is worth while to mention the lay-out of the water-garden. I am often asked whether it is simply a garden with a stream running through it? The O.E.D. quotes from *The Naturalist on the Thames* (1902) by Charles J. Cornish. "A recent addition to the country house is the 'water-garden', in which a running brook is the centre and *motif* of the subsidiary ornaments of flowers, ferns, trees, shrubs and mosses." We could scarcely improve upon that. The running water is constantly clean and therefore provides a healthy moist soil for the plants (such as the Gunneras), which do best with their roots (but not their crowns) submerged. A narrow channel can be made to carry the water to a pool where Water-lilies may be planted. They need still water, although they often do well in backwaters of rivers.

Further, a form of irrigation can be adopted to make a bog-garden where many moisture-loving things will thrive. (Both the yellow and the white white Bog Arums grow in swampy ground at the Windsor Gardens.)

If you have a small pool, it is possible to make a miniature water-garden by using it to supply an artificial ditch or a channel with water, tiny moisture-loving plants like *Primula rosea* and *Gunnera magellanica* being grown along the sides. The ditch, which may connect with another pool or terminate at a flagged pathway, must of course be lined with cement and come a little below the level of the pool so that the overflow keeps the soil wet. *Gunnera magellanica*, incidentally, is the smallest species, with leaves only two and a half inches across, and a rampant creeper.

The most famous is the gargantuan *G. manicata*, whose leaves in the warm southern regions of these islands have a spread of nine feet and whose stems attain a height of eight feet or more. In the Isle of Wight I have seen mature specimens covering a space thirty feet wide; most of them had twenty to thirty leaves, and the crowns of some were as large as a man's body. The stems carrying the flowers were cut back as soon as they appeared in order to promote the strong healthy growth of the foliage. A native of Southern Brazil, it was introduced in 1867.

G. chilensis is less of a giant than the preceding species, its leaves measuring about five feet across, its stems from three to six feet tall. And it is less prickly than the other; in many gardens it is easily damaged by wind. (All the big Gunneras should be given a place sheltered from high winds.)

A rich loamy soil is necessary for them and an abundance of water, of course—especially during the growing season. The crowns must be set a foot or two above the water so that they are dry in the winter. They often suffer irreparable damage if stagnant moisture collects round them in frosty weather. The easiest way to propagate these plants is by root-division in early April.

Rheums are another class of foliage plants

suitable for growing near water; they are commonly known as the Ornamental Rhubarb, *Rheum rhaponticum* being the species from which the edible garden kinds are derived. It could be used as a foliage plant; in fact it sometimes is. But other species with larger, darker green leaves (beautifully divided) are more decorative. And some are used, too, in borders in the garden proper, where, with their broad handsome leaves (some with a copper sheen), and tall spikes of flowers they make an arresting group. *R. palmatum* 'Bowles' Crimson', in the sculptural quality of its leaves and the elegance of its tall-stemmed flowers, eclipses any other herbaceous perennial grown near it. In full bloom (July), when the five-foot stems are topped with crimson flowers, it can hold its own in the watergarden with any of the Gunneras. (I consider var. *atrosanguineum*, with leaves three feet wide and very dark red flowers, equally handsome.)

These Rheums thrive gloriously in moist waterside soil but are often grown in a border which is made up of rich, leafy, well-dug loam.

I like *R. emodi*, from the Himalayas, with its coppery-tinged foliage and tall flower-stems (up to ten feet high). A fine stately plant for growing near water. It does well at the Savill Gardens. Its deeply divided leaves are copper-coloured at first, then they become a dark, burnished green and are pink on the undersides. The conspicuous yellow veins add much to their beauty. The Rhubarb-like stems are pink with a bloom on them; and the sheath containing the leaf is carmine-pink: altogether a fine ornamental plant.

R. nobile is also from the Himalayas and has bright glossy green leaves with red veins and stalks. It grows about three feet tall.

The official Rhubarb is derived from *R. officinale* (prepared from the rhizomes, the powder being a yellowish brown colour); but the plant is also a good ornamental, with its lobed green leaves and tall, green, feathery flower panicles.

Specimens of the genus *Rodgersia* also grow in the damp, open woodlands at Windsor. In April you can see the dark brown, horse-chestnut-shaped leaves of *R. aesculifolia* coming up; and later, when they are opened out, they give a magnificent show of rich colour, especially against a background of green lacy Ferns. For the water-garden, it is one of the best of the moderate-sized foliage plants—though it does sometimes reach a height of six feet in warm peaty soils. The leaflets, seven in number, measure from four to ten inches long. Its flowers come in upright panicles from one to two feet long and are creamy white.

R. podophylla is from three to four feet tall as a rule, but will go up to a much greater height in warm climates when it is grown in rich deep soil near water. The feathery, greenish white flowers resemble those of the *Astilbes*, to which the genus is related. Those of *R. podophylla* do not last as long, but it is a plant we grow for its foliage. The leaves are finger-shaped, the five leaflets being five to ten inches long and three to six inches wide; they are light green in spring and take on a striking metallic sheen during the summer months. Deep rich peaty soil gives the finest plants.

There are *R. pinnata* and its different forms; and *R. tabularis*, whose flowers perhaps more resemble those of the *Astilbes* than any of the others.

R. pinnata rubra, I consider the best red variety; var. *superba* (pale rose) is taller and more striking, the inflorescence being almost

Lysichitum americanum

Osmunda regalis

Coleus

Zebrina pendula

Begonia rex (exotic foliage plant)

Gunnera manicata

Yucca filamentosa

Nymphaea (water lily)

two feet long. The leaves are made up of five to nine leaflets, which are six to eight inches long and make a very handsome leaf.

R. tabularis has rounded leaves (the specific epithet means table-like) and pretty cream-white flowers. Rodgersias may be propagated by root-division or by seed.

Bamboos: the word evokes the jungles and tropical regions of the East. They are the giant grasses that flourish luxuriantly in a humid atmosphere and rich, festering leaf soil. And those we grow in this country do best in the moist peaty loams of the waterside. The genuine Bamboos (*Bambusa*) can be cultivated only in our hothouses—*Bambusa vulgaris striata* is one; it is described in the *Botanical Magazine* (t,6079), Vol. 30 (1874). "The specimen at Kew, sent from the Calcutta Botanical Garden, is about six feet high, but Lindley describes it as attaining twenty feet, which from its habit it may well be supposed to do. . . . This plant flowered in November last, with Mr. Bull, who kindly sent me the specimen here figured, its anthers stain paper of a lilac colour. . . ."

The numerous species have now been divided into several genera: *Arundinaria* and *Phyllo-*

stachys are the two best known and contain some of the finest hardy kinds offered for sale by our nurseries.

Both genera have distinguishing characters. In the *Arundinaria* the stems, which are cylindrical and straight, have numerous branches coming from a single joint; whereas in the *Phyllostachys* there are only two or three; and the stems are flattened on one side above the joints or internodes.

In the wild some of the Bamboos attain heights of sixty or eighty feet or more but under cultivation, at least in this country, the tallest is probably not more than thirty feet. One of the most widely planted is *Arundinaria japonica* commonly known as the Japanese Metake. It is hardy enough for many gardens and in the south is sometimes utilised for wind-breaks, though normally Bamboos themselves need sheltering from drying winds. Its leaves are eight to twelve inches long and about one and a half inches wide, the upper surface glossy green, the undersides slightly glaucous. A graceful Bamboo, reaching a height of ten or fifteen feet, but much taller in the South of France. The stem-sheaths, as in many species of this genus, are very persistent. It is seen at its best when grown in an isolated clump on the edge of a stream and it thrives in town gardens. Siebold introduced the species from Japan, its native habitat, over a hundred years ago.

Most nurseries who sell it recommend it for smallish gardens, since it is of tufted habit and doesn't spread far as do so many of the Bamboos.

A. nitida is a Chinese species with slender stems, not much thicker than a pencil, and needs partial shade as it soon suffers when exposed to full sun. The stems, crowded, are black-purple in colour and attain a height of six to ten feet; the leaves are two to three inches long and about half an inch wide, shining green above and pale and glaucous beneath. A charming delicate-looking Bamboo, but completely hardy around London, its stems are erect and leafless the first year but become arching and leafy the following season. I would choose it before any other Bamboo, I think, for growing in the water-garden. The species was introduced into Britain via St. Petersburg in 1889.

A. palmata is said to be the most common Bamboo we grow in this country. Although of moderate height (six to eight feet tall), it cannot

73

be recommended for limited space, for it is a rampant spreader, its underground stems shooting up often several feet away from the parent clump. But its large leaves, thirteen inches long and about three inches wide, make it one of the most handsome of the exotic-looking foliage plants for the waterside. The leaves are bright green above and glaucous beneath, but after a few years begin to lose their fresh green colour; the old stems should then be cut back to ground level in May; the young shoots springing up again very quickly and producing new juicy green growths and foliage. The species was introduced from Japan, its habitat, in 1889. (Botanists now describe the plant under *Sasa senanensis*: *sasa* is the Japanese word for dwarf Bamboos.)

The largest-leaved hardy Bamboo we grow is *A. ragamowskii*, a native of China and cultivated in our gardens before the middle of the nineteenth century. Some of the leaves are eighteen inches long and four inches wide in the middle, dark green above and glaucous beneath. This species is seldom more than four feet high and has hollow stems about an eighth of an inch in diameter, the joints coming one inch to three inches apart. Like the preceding plant, it spreads rapidly by creeping root-stocks and, like that species, is now mostly described under the genus *Sasa*, the specific name being *Sasa tessellata*.

A magnificent plant, with its ribbon-shaped leaves, for fringing a pool or for growing on the bank of a stream, it has never been known to flower in this country.

It is worth while to mention here the flowering of Bamboos. Many die some time after they once flower, while others are badly crippled but eventually recover. Yet others produce a certain number of shoots which flower and then perish, the non-flowering ones remaining active and healthy. After some years it often happens, however, that all the stems flower simultaneously, then the whole plant dies. Gardeners have found that it is possible to save the life of a Bamboo by immediately cutting back to ground level those stems that show signs of flowering.

Another interesting fact is that the plants belonging to one species wherever they are growing — in the wild, or under cultivation in hot-houses — all flower (and then perish) simultaneously.

The genus *Phyllostachys* is similarly rich in handsome Bamboos suitable for the water-garden.

My first choice is *Phyllostachys viridi-glaucescens*, which is a vigorous species attaining a height of eighteen feet in warm districts. (It has not yet flowered under cultivation apparently.) The stems are hollow, about three-quarters of an inch in diameter, of a yellow-green colour, purplish at the joints, the outer ones arching gracefully outward and touching the ground. Growing near the bank of a stream, they will touch the water. The leaves, bright green above and glaucous beneath, are small, narrow and pointed. Hillier's catalogue describes it as: "A vigorous, very hardy Chinese species and one of the most adaptable under cultivation. Canes fifteen to twenty feet, bright green tinged purple at the nodes, becoming yellowish green the second year".

I would not of course grow it in a small garden; it takes up a great amount of space; moreover it is inclined to run. (On the whole the *Phyllostachys* do not spread so rapidly as the *Arundinaria*.)

The Black-stemmed Bamboo is *P. nigra*, a native of China and Japan and one of the most striking on account of its handsome stems, which grow up to twenty feet tall in the warm south. Around London they are often not more than eight or ten feet, and about half an inch in diameter. The leaves, two to four inches long and a half to three-quarters of an inch wide, come in plumose masses, their dark green colour looking particularly beautiful against the long black stems. Hillier's catalogue quotes it: "This beautiful black-stemmed species flowered and died almost everywhere, but a few survived in one or two places, and we are again able to offer a few plants". The species, a native of China and Japan, was the first of the *Phyllostachys* to be grown in this country.

P. henonsis. Nurseries commend it, and gardeners I know who have grown it for years acclaim it the finest Bamboo in cultivation in this country. In a rich moist soil and a warm sheltered place, it is gloriously luxuriant with its plumose masses of dark, shining green foliage. The stems reach a height of fourteen feet and arch outward. The leaves are from two to four inches in length and about half an inch wide and retain their lovely colour till winter.

Its native country is Japan, from where it was introduced in 1890. Specimens cultivated in Britain began flowering in 1900 and five years later every one was either dead or severely crippled; some, however, did recover, and from these new stocks were built up.

As already mentioned, Bamboos like a site sheltered from cold searing winds, and many prefer shade to full sun. (They prosper exceedingly in clearings in woodland, the trees affording adequate protection.) A mulch of sifted peat or leaf mould applied in April is beneficial, keeping the soil moist. From spring to early summer, when they shed their old leaves, they are least attractive; but the fresh sharp green growth begins to shoot out in late summer, and the plants are beautiful then through the autumn and the winter.

Bamboos are for the most part tall airy graceful plants that sway and flutter in the wind; but the *Lysichitums* are the most solid of all our foliage plants: dumpy when the Arum lily-like spathes begin to unfurl and perhaps more curious then than beautiful. The lemon-yellow colour is bright and very conspicuous on the banks of a stream, where the plant is usually grown; it needs a permanently moist soil. As soon as the spathe fades, the leaves grow taller and have the appearance of thick giant Spinach-leaves, the largest three feet long and one and a half feet wide. They stand erect, and the mid-ribs are wide and prominent. The spadix, the fleshy spike that forms later and carries the minute closely packed flowers, is quite ornamental and from the seeds new plants can be raised.

Lysichitum americanum is the yellow-flowered type mostly seen in water-gardens and is a native of Western North America. The white *L. camtschatcense* is much rarer: attractive on its own, but eclipsed by the bright yellow colour of the other. In fact it is best not to grow the two close together. The white has a wider distribution; it is a native of Kamtschatka, Japan; E. Siberia and of California and other States on the Pacific seaboard.

Both species are perfectly hardy and most readily propagated by root-division. From the unpleasant smell of the flowers no doubt the popular name 'Skunk Cabbage' has arisen. In some parts of the country I have heard the plants called the 'Stink Cabbage'.

Iris foetidissima is the 'Stinking Gladwin' (or Gladdon, the name coming from the Latin *gladiolus*, Sword-lily). The leaves have an unpleasant smell when they are broken. They are stiff and an attractive shade of green, and provide an especially good contrast with the broad, shining green leaves of the *Lysichitum*. This Iris, a native of Britain, is an inhabitant of moist shady places; its flowers, which come in June, are small and of a dull bluish lilan colour; they do not last long.

The sword-shaped leaves of our Yellow Flag-iris (*Iris pseudacorus*) are somewhat bigger, and the plant is altogether more attractive than the other. It is common along the banks of the Thames, where it often grows in shallow water in the company of Reeds and Rushes. The leaves are two to three feet tall, one inch wide and a pleasant glaucous-green colour.

I have seen it growing in a large clump in clear shallow water and next to it the pink-flowered Rush *Butomus umbellatus*, which is native to Britain. They make a lovely association for the waterside. Behind them on the bank, with its roots going down deep into the moist soil, *Hosta glauca* provides the right kind of contrast: its blue-green leaves are broad and spread out into a low mass over the ground.

For grouping together on the banks of a stream, Hostas are ideal foliage plants. Where space is limited, use the miniature *H. minor* var. *alba* (from Japan), whose leaves are about six inches long and one and a half inches wide.

H. ventricosa var. *marginata* has fresh green heart-shaped leaves margined with white; they are about nine inches long and eight inches wide and have stalks measuring often more than nine inches in length.

H. rectifolia has leaves twelve inches long, more or less erect; it is a good plant for massing behind those species with recurved leaves, these being seen to best advantage when planted on the edge of a stream. Often their lowest leaves will touch the water.

There is a long list of foliage plants suitable for the water-garden. Many nurseries supply catalogues of herbaceous perennials, which include a special selection of hardy aquatics and bog plants. Hillier quotes about thirty genera. The Sweet Flag is *Acorus calamus*, which has sword-shaped leaves, two to three feet long and a quarter to three-quarters of an inch wide; when they are bruised they give off a pleasant smell of cinnamon, hence the popular name.

The type plant is less often seen, though, than the variety *variegatus*, whose leaves are striped a deep yellow; it turns a paler colour in late summer. The miniature *Acorus gramineus*

81

variegatus is a good choice for a damp situation in the rockery (*page 50*). These ornamental Grasses can be grown in shallow water or in rich moist soils.

Water Hawthorn is an appropriate name for the aquatic *Aponogeton distachyus*, for it has pure white flowers with a scent reminiscent of the spring-blooming Hawthorn. The *Aponogeton* is a floating plant with bright green oblong, longish leaves and can be grown in water to a depth of two to four feet — either indoors (two feet will suffice) or out of doors.

Even more handsome are the floating leaves of the variety *Lagrangei*; these are green above and violet underneath.

Cyperus longus is sometimes called the Galingale, which is the Sedge, whose roots are, or were, used in cookery. This perennial Rush or Grass is a native of Britain; it is about four feet tall, with very attractive reddish brown spikelets at the end of the Rush-like stems. It is particularly effective growing in water in front of the large-leaved Gunneras.

Another charming floating plant for a still stretch of water is *Myriophyllum proserpinacoides*, known as the Parrot's Feather, which has delicate feathery green foliage on stems protruding eight inches or so from the water. The plant is offered by Hillier.

The finest of all the floating plants are of course the Water-lilies and these are naturally grown for their flowers; but the leaves of some are very beautiful: in the variety 'William Falconer', for instance, they are a purplish copper; and 'Rose Arey' has rich purplish leaves which turn deep green later in the year.

CHAPTER VI

Foliage Plants with Shrubs

MANY gardeners say that shrubs do not need the company of foliage plants. They have in mind, no doubt, flowering-shrubs like the hybrid evergreen Rhododendrons and Camellias, whose foliage is attractive all through the year.

Personally I consider the glaucous leaves of *Rhododendron concatenans* as decorative as those of many plants which are grown specifically for their foliage. Like the rest of the genus, its flowering-season is short — at the most a week or two — and we enjoy the beauty of its leaves practically all the year round.

The Japanese Maples (*Acer palmatum* and its varieties) are essentially foliage shrubs. Their finely cut leaves, some as delicate-looking as Ferns, are wonderfully decorative. And colour is provided in spring and summer by the red- or copper-leaved varieties like *Acer palmatum dissectum atropurpureum*, which is first red then later turns a brighter, glowing red. A clearing in a woodland is the best place for these Maples and set against the thick lichened trunks of Beeches or Oaks they make a beautiful picture.

But there are one or two shrubs — Laurel and Box, for example — which can be made more interesting by growing certain foliage plants with them.

The common Box (*Buxus sempervirens*) responds well to clipping and is the next best thing to Yew for topiary-work. A specimen clipped into an elaborate shape is usually set somewhere on its own: it needs no companion plants; but a simple hemisphere is an ideally contrasting shape for the broad recurved leaves of the Hosta. (This association was mentioned in *Chapter I, page 19*).

Sword-shaped leaves, those of the *Iris* in particular, provide an even more striking contrast. I think the best to plant behind a hemispherically shaped Box shrub is the tall hybrid *Iris* $\times$ *ochraurea*, whose leaves, grey-green and narrow, reach a height of four feet or so. And in front, *I. pumila*, with leaves up to nine inches long, is as good as any of the dwarf kinds.

One of the most picturesque uses of Box I have

ever come across was when a closely clipped mound of it was surrounded by a double row of the exotic *Begonia rex*. The plants were in a large round bed in the middle of a shady paved walk.

It is as a background plant that Box is mostly valued, and as a low hedge it shows up well the beauty of white- and silver-leaved foliage plants, though not so startlingly as does black-green Yew.

The white-leaved *Senecio greyii* (*laxifolius*) grown against Yew is thought too hard a contrast by many gardeners. But I like to see the plant and the Lavender Cotton set against a low Box hedge. The foliage of the latter assumes a more intense silver-white colour when the plant is grown in a light sandy soil. Like the Senecio, it gives the best results when it is raised from cuttings every autumn; the new plants should be set out fairly close together in the early spring.

Polygonum sachalinense is a giant perennial with huge roughly heart-shaped green leaves (some a foot long) and reddish fleshy stems up to ten feet tall. I saw it first in the University Botanic Garden at Oxford where it was planted in one of the foliage borders but had spread far, some of the suckers shooting up on the

86

surrounding lawn.

It is one of the best plants for growing with Laurel: set right in front of a large specimen, which will show up its handsome stems and foliage and incidentally help to control it — at least from behind; the suckers that come up in front should be dug up before they spread too far. (This Polygonum is most suitable for woodlands where it can run freely and perhaps come up against plants like the vigorous Bamboos, which are a match for it.)

Nothing could be better to grow with the rather ugly Laurel than Bamboos, either the spreading kinds or the tufted. It is possible to keep this shrub low-growing by an annual drastic pruning; and, at about four feet high and making a dense mound of glossy green foliage, it provides a handsome groundwork for tall Bamboos to spring from. On the other hand, it can be allowed to grow up tall, fifteen feet or more, and used as a background; the yellow-stemmed species of *Arundinaria*, such as *Arundinaria nobile*, with graceful, golden-yellow stems, will stand out conspicuously against the glossy-green.

That exotic-looking shrub *Cephalotaxus fortunei*, with leaves like those of the Yew, only much larger, is sometimes planted in conjunction with the equally exotic-looking Fern called *Blechnum tabulare*. This is listed by most nurseries as a greenhouse species; but I have seen it growing, though not actually flourishing, in gardens near London. (Both the *Cephalotaxus*, Chinese Plum-yew, and the *Blechnum* may be seen in the Savill Gardens, Windsor; but they are not planted together.)

The fronds or leaves of this Fern are about two feet long and eight inches wide; of a dark coppery green colour and of a metallic wiry-looking texture. The plants prosper in a mixture of two parts leaf mould, one part loam and one part sand. For sub-tropical effects it is ideal. Both plants like partial shade.

Although, as I stated at the beginning of this chapter, evergreen Rhododendrons do not need the company of foliage plants, occasionally the hardy Maindenhair-fern, *Adiantum pedatum* var. Klondyke is massed as a foreground plant to dwarfer kinds like the glossy green, small-leaved *Rhododendron* × *praecox*. This *Adiantum* is one of the loveliest Ferns, revelling in part woodland and in early spring producing delicate-looking feathery fronds tinged with carmine-pink.

And the hybrid Rhododendron provides a perfect background for it. This shrub may on rare occasions come into flower in April when the pink fronds are showing up well; though normally, if the winter has been mild, it will have bloomed in February, the faded flowers will have fallen and the young fresh evergreen foliage will be at its best.

The evergreen Camellias, especially the variants of *camellia japonica*, also provide a beautiful background to this elegant Fern. The glossy leaves are larger than those of the Rhododendron and the pink or white flowers, single or double, are in full bloom in April. Nothing could be better as a foil to these exotic blooms than this hardy Maindenhair-fern. Lovely outside, but perhaps lovelier when they are picked for indoor decoration.

CHAPTER VII

A Choice of Foliage Plants

SPECIES and varieties of 100-odd genera are described in this chapter. It would be an easy matter to mention twice the number, but it is not possible to include more in a book this size. Most of those listed here will no doubt be known to lovers of foliage plants (certainly to collectors). The half-hardy and the tender ones may be seen in the formal beds of our public gardens; if not there, then in florists' show-windows. And a few of the more exotic ones some of us grow in pots on our window-sills.

Acaena, a genus of hardy dwarf perennials, is represented in our gardens mostly by the species. *A. buchananii* and *A. microphylla*. Both are natives of New Zealand. The first, which was named to commemorate John Buchanan, a student of New Zealand flora, is a little carpeting plant, with silver-green silky leaves about three-quarters of an inch long, made up of minute leaflets. An ideal plant for covering rocks (often spreading far), or it can be used as a groundwork for spring-flowering bulbs.

A. microphylla (small leaved). Its tiny leaves vary in colour from grey to bronze. This species may be similarly used in the rockery or in the woodland; it likes sunny or shady moist places. In summer it carries red spiny flowers in close heads.

Both plants prosper in ordinary, well-drained soils and may be propagated by division or by cuttings. The generic name is from the Greek word *akaina*, meaning a thorn; it refers to the hooked fruit.

The genus *Acanthus* contains several species which are often utilised for sub-tropical garden effects. *A. mollis* (soft; referring to the downy flower-spikes) has finely cut, heart-shaped leaves (two feet long, one foot wide), which are the plant's chief attraction — at least for the best part of the year. The flowers, red or white, come in spikes (eighteen inches long) in late summer.

I prefer the variety *A. mollis latifolius* (broad-leaved), which is larger and more robust. For sub-tropical garden effects the flowers should be cut off. Small plants of *A. mollis* may be grown in pots or boxes for window decoration.

A. spinosus (spiny; referring to the leaves). This is the classic plant mentioned in the introduction; the beauty of the foliage inspired the Greek, Callimachus. Like *A. mollis*, it is from three to four feet tall. Its leaves are beautifully divided, the divisions spiny. An herbaceous perennial, which is particularly striking massed behind an edging of one of the large-leaved Hostas, say, *Hosta glauca.*

The species of Acanthus described here need a deep loamy soil and give the best results in a sunny situation. (Although *H. glauca* prefers partial shade, it will succeed in sunny places, provided it is given a deep rich leafy soil.) Propagation is best by root-division in spring or early autumn. The plants are natives of Southern Europe.

Acanthus is from the Greek *akanthos* (spine); the name referring to the spiny character of the leaves of some species.

Achillea clavenae (in honour of the Italian apothecary Chiavena, the name latinised into Clavena). This soft-leaved hoary plant is a native of the Eastern Alps and a treasure for the rock-garden. It is of tufted habit and has deeply divided leaves. A little silvery foliage plant and a parent of several good hybrid forms.

Achillea is the Latin name of a plant, probably the same as *Achilleos*, which was named after Achilles, who is said to have discovered the medicinal properties of the plant. It is no doubt our native Milfoil, *Achillea millefolium*, found wild in many parts of Europe. William Langham mentions it in *The Garden of Health* (1579): "Milfoile or Yarrow: The decoction thereof doth cure the bloudy flixe and all other lasks".

A. clypeolata. A species with the same mat-forming habit and growth as *A. millefolium*, and regarded as one of the loveliest of all the Ahilleas, is *A. clypeolata*. It has finely dissected, feather-like leaves, silvery grey in colour, and small yellow flowers. A good choice for growing with the Cheddar Pink.

Acorus (from *Akoros*, an ancient Greek name for a plant with an aromatic rhizome). *A. calamus* var. *variegatus* as a decorative foliage plant. The leaves of the variety are striped cream and yellow. This plant, I think, vies with any of the waterside Irises we grow for their foliage.

The variegated dwarf *A. gramineus* (grass-like) *variegatus* is similarly a more suitable garden plant than the type. It is densely tufted in habit, the narrow leaves being eight inches tall and striped with white.

The variety *pusillus* (very small) seldom goes above two inches in height. An excellent miniature for edging part of a small pool.

Acorus may be grown in shallow water or in moist loamy soil and are propagated by division during the early spring. (Although I have seen these dwarfs grown as edging-plants in an herbaceous border, they prove troublesome there because of their habit of spreading.)

Adiantum pedatum, Klondyke variety, belongs to the Maidenhair fern family (*pedatum* refers to the pedate or compound leaves). I have seldom come across it in our gardens. It may be seen in botanical collections, however; it is growing on rock-work at the Savill Gardens, Windsor, where, by the way, I first saw a specimen one April some years ago. It has blackish-brown wiry stems, eighteen inches long, and copper-pink Fern-like leaves in early spring.

It needs a sandy peaty soil such as is to be found in woodlands. Outside the woodland-garden it is difficult to establish, unless its rhizomes are well covered by coarse leaf mould or leaves through the winter. If it is grown in a rockery, it should be planted at the foot of a shady boulder.

It is an exquisite medium-sized Fern for a pot and should be kept in a temperature of about 55°F. through the winter.

Habitat: North America, Japan, China and the Himalayas.

A. capillus-veneris (Venus's Hair) is the Maindenhair-fern. It is widely diffused over the globe, and is found growing in the shady crevices of caves in the warm, maritime parts of Southern England. Elsewhere it would no doubt succumb to frosts. The only way we can grow it in our gardens is to sink it in its pot near a shady boulder when the cold weather is past. It must be lifted again about the end of October and grown on indoors. Its dainty, elegant foliage is well known and prized as a foil to many hothouse flowers. The rhizome must always be on the surface of the soil, which should consist of equal parts of coarse peat, silver sand and sifted leaf mould.

Both species may be increased by root-division.

Adiantum comes from the word *adiantos*, remaining dry. When the fronds, or leaves, are dipped into water they are unwetted when taken out.

Aira capillaris (hair-like, very slender; referring to the stems). An annual ornamental Grass, quite uncommon in our gardens, but deserving a place there, say, in the front row of a flower-border, for the silvery spikelets it carries in open panicles during May and June. It is of tufted habit, with hair-like stems up to fifteen inches in height. The panicles are about three inches long and wide, the tiny silvery spikelets coming on long stalks. A graceful delicate-looking Grass, which is raised from seed sown in a light soil during the spring. It likes partial shade. When cut and dried, this Grass is an ideally charming foil to Everlastings like *Helichrysum bracteatum*, which has prickly, yellow or orange flowers.

Aira is the Greek name of *Lolium temulentum*, Quivering Grass.

Ajuga reptans (creeping) *atropurpurea* is the bronzy purple-leaved 'Bugle', which grows quickly in cool moist soil and has pretty blue flower-spikes in spring. The leaves are from two to three inches long and form a pleasing, purplish mat. The colour retains its purplish glow even in the deepest shade. Plant it in the woodland-garden or in a shady corner of the rockery.

Alchemilla (from the Arabic name of the plant: *Alkemelych*). *A. alpina* (of the mountains). Grow this in the rockery too. The undersides of the leaves are silky white; they are roundish, about two inches wide and usually seven foliolate. In summer the plant has tiny greenish flowers. It is about six inches high and when massed gives a delightful show of silver-white. Ordinary sandy soil suits it best.

A. vulgaris (common). Its popular name is the Lady's Mantle. The garden forms of it (*A. mollis* and *A. major*) have broad, soft velvety leaves and large sprays of yellow-green flowers.

Grow them in the front row of the border, where they can show off their attractive leaves. The plants like a well-drained loamy soil.

Allium karataviense (of the Kara Tau Mts., East Russia). The plant belongs to the Onion or Garlic family (*Allium* is an old Latin name for Garlic), several species of which are grown in the flower-border. Our plant grows about eight inches tall and has broad, flat glaucous-green leaves which are often beautifully variegated. It is well adapted for edging or for growing in a pocket in the rockery, and has white flower-heads which bloom during the summer. Propagate the plant by offsets or by the bulbils in the inflorescence.

The plant is figured in the *Botanical Magazine*, Vol.35 (1879), but the leaves are not variegated; they are blue-green above and glaucous beneath. It is described as being: "one of the recent discoveries of the Russian explorers in Central Asia. It was first found several years ago by Sewerzow and Krausel in the Karatau Mountains, east of Samarcand, and was gathered again in the summer of 1876 on the Alatau range by Dr. Albert Regel, who sent bulbs to his father at St. Petersburg, from whom we received it".

Alternanthera ('alternate anthers', which in most species are barren). These are the gorgeously coloured foliage plants whose bizarre markings perhaps limit their use to formal bedding. Gardeners choose them not only for their vivid colourings, but because they respond well to clipping and can thus, in ribbon-planting, be kept down to a few inches in height. They are all tender and must be lifted before the frosts come.

A. amoena (pleasing) is the dwarfest, and has leaves one to three inches long, ovalish in shape; their colour underneath is green but they are strikingly marked with red and orange. Of the variants it has produced, *rosea* and *spectabilis* are two of the best known.

A. bettzichiana is rather tall and occasionally used as a pot-plant in formal beds. Its green and red leaves contrast strikingly with any silver or grey foliage. The plant has produced many variants, some of dwarf habit, such as var. *paronychioides*, which is about four inches tall and has deep orange-red leaves shaded dark green; and var. *spathulata* (six to eight inches tall), with red leaves shaded coppery green.

These bedders need a rich, light soil and must be grown in full sun. Gardeners propagate them by cuttings taken in spring. They are rooted, of course, in a heated greenhouse.

Many of the species are now described by botanists under the genus *Telanthera*.

Alyssum saxatile variegatum (growing among rocks). The popular name is Gold Dust; and I have heard it called Golden Tuft and Basket-of-Gold. This variegated form is less often seen than the type plant. When in flower, they look the same, the hanging masses of bright yellow flowers practically hiding the leaves. These are hoary downy and grey-green in the type plant, but beautifully variegated yellow and grey-green in the other. During the autumn, when the faded flowers have been removed, they are very conspicuous seen against the weathered surface of stone-work.

The plant flourishes in full sun and in any ordinary light sandy soil and is easily propagated by cuttings taken in early summer. It is a native of Southern Europe.

Antennaria. The alpine species we grow here are silvery-leaved carpeting-plants which are used in rock-gardens and Alpine Lawns. The different forms of *A. dioica* can be bought at many nurseries and are regarded by those who grow them as some of the loveliest. (The specific epithet *dioica* refers to the dioecious nature of the plants: they have the unisexual male and female flowers on separate plants.)

The form called *hyperborea* (northern) is about two inches high and has silver leaves and pink flowers; *minima* is a smaller kind; and *tomen -tosum* (covered with thick down) is a stronger grower than the other two; the silver colouring of its foliage is more pronounced; the flowers are white, on stems about five inches high.

These carpeting-plants are natives of Europe, Asia and North America. They thrive in poor sandy soil and are quickly propagated by division in spring.

Antennaria is derived from *antennae*: the pappus on the male flowers resembles a butterfly's antennae.

Aponogeton distachyus (with two branches; referring to the forked inflorescence). The Water Hawthorn or Cape Pondweed, a native of South Africa. The Hawthorn-scented white flowers and oblong, bright green leaves (three to six inches long) float on the water and are decorative all the summer. It is obtainable from Messrs. Hillier, who describe it as having pure, waxen white, fragrant flowers and floating leaves. Some years ago it could be bought for 15 pence.

Arenaria balearica (from the Balearic Islands) is the Creeping Sandwort, which covers moist shady rocks with bright moss-green, tiny leaves, and in spring is dotted over with minute white starry flowers. Fairy-like and delicate-looking, they dislike the sun. There are perhaps only a few gardens where the plant will succeed for long, for the soil must never at any time become dry. It is most easily accommodated by the side of a shady pool surrounded by low rocks. The soil should be a sandy, peaty loam. Propagation is by division of the plant in September.

Arenaria is derived from *arena*, sand (many of the species thrive in sandy soils).

Arisaema candidissimum (white and shining). It is related to the Arum family, to which our Cuckoo-pint of the woods belongs. The handsome leaves are three foliolate, the leaflets being three to eight inches long and as wide; the spathe, or flower, is white and sometimes tinged with rose. A native of West China and completely hardy. Grow it in the woodland- or the semi-wild-garden and plant it in deep loamy soil.

A. consanguineum, found wild in different parts of temperate East Asia and Yunnan, China, is not as hardy and needs a sheltered spot in the rock-garden for the sake of its large divided leaves.

These plants do well in sun or shade and are easily increased by root-division.

Armeria. From *Flos Armeriae*, the Latin name of the flowers of a *Dianthus*, probably the Sweet William, which in the O.E.D. is described amongst other names: "the Deptford Pink, *D. armeria* (also called Sweet-William. Catchfly)". The popular name of the Armeria is Thrift or Sea Pink.

A perennial 'ribbon' foliage effect can be had by planting *Armeria maritima* or its varieties and one of the Dianthus, such as the Cheddar Pink, in long rows close together. The plants should be allowed to grow freely, of course, and not be trimmed up as in formal 'ribbon-planting'. The dark green grass-like leaves of the *Armeria* combined with the blue-grey of the Pink provide a valuable drift of colour through the winter months. *A. maritima* (growing by the sea) has produced several varieties; the best known is *A. maritima laucheana*, a very tufted variety — a favourite Thrift for edging; var. *variegata* has golden-yellow foliage all through the winter.

A. montana (of the mountains) is a miniature species and suitable for rockeries and sink-gardens. I have had it in a shallow pan indoors through the winter; its fresh green grass-like foliage is very welcome then.

Arrhenatherum (from the Greek *arren,* male; and *ather,* awn; referring to the awned staminate flower). There is apparently only one variety offered by nurseries and that is *A. elatius* (tall) *bulbosum variegatum.* It is grown as an edging to borders at the University Botanic Garden, Oxford. A dwarf ornamental Grass, green with white stripes, which spreads quickly, forming large clumps. But it can be controlled by pulling it up (the rooted pieces are planted out in spring when one wants to propagate it). It grows well in loamy soil and in the flower-border is best used as an edging. Its spreading habit would make it a nuisance if it were planted among perennials.

Artemisia. (The word comes from *Artemis*, which was one of the names of the Greek Goddess, Diana.) A species of *Artemisia* (probably the Southernwood) was described by John de Trevisa in a work he translated from the Latin in 1398. "Artemisisa is callyd moder (mother) of herbes and was somtyme halowed to the goddesse that hyghte (was called) Arthemis."

Several species which are essentially foliage plants are offered by nurseries; and the one most frequently grown is *A. abrotanum* (the Latin word for Southernwood). It has other popular names, viz. Lad's Love and Old Man.

Its feathery silvery green foliage is at its best in early summer and makes a pleasing foil to the hardy Lilies (*Lilium*). A clump of *Lilium regale* looks particularly well behind a row of it or set in small groups among the plants, which should be grown about four feet apart. This shrubby

Artemisia may be similarly grown with the Madonna Lily (*L. candidum*) and will help to hide the leaves, which so often begin to shrivel and turn brown before the flowers are fully open.

The Southernwood is about three feet tall and may be damaged sometimes by frost in cold exposed places. Its fragrant foliage smells strongest after a summer shower.

Artemisia arborescens (becoming tree-like). A species of shrubby habit but not a tall plant — seldom more than three feet high. The leaves, about two inches long, are finely dissected, silky and silvery white. Like the Southernwood, it is damaged sometimes by frosts in exposed gardens; and for the sake of its foliage it should be covered up during the winter. In sheltered gardens it is unharmed. The epithet *arborescens* is perhaps misleading, but it refers probably to the erect, woody shoots. Grow it on the edge of a woodland; in the wild-garden — mass it — or in a shady part of the herbaceous border. Both species like a light loamy soil.

A. frigida (cold; perhaps referring to the hoary appearance of the foliage). This is another shrubby species, between ten and twenty inches tall, with finely dissected silvery leaves, which accord well with pale mauves and pinks in the flower-border.

It would be interesting to know the name of the Artemisia described in Vol. 9 of *The New Flora and Silva* (1937): "An Artemisia, which I owe to Mr. Bowles; its name has not yet been found, but it is surely the most indestructible of its family. The grey leaves give a new colour note in the shade, and as for propagation, you merely pull off a piece and push it in the ground and there you are. In shade it seldom flowers but makes a dwarf rounded bush: in sun it throws up long spikes of pale yellow flowers in autumn, which, though not floral, are architectural".

There are three taller kinds, which I like to see grown as foil plants in the herbaceous border. *A. lactiflora* (milk-white flowers), with erect stems about four feet tall, and pinnate leaves eight inches long, the leaflets being one to three inches long and pale underneath. The panicles of white flowers intensify the whiteness of the plant. The common name of this handsome border plant is the White Mugwort. It is a native of China and India.

A. ludoviciana (of Louisiana, U.S.A.). This is the White Sage of the Deep South, a choice white downy-leaved plant for the front row of a border. It is from two to four feet high and in summer has small brownish-yellow flowers.

A. purshiana (named for F. T. Pursh, 1774-1820, a German botanist who researched in the U.S.A. and wrote an important work on its flora). It has stems two to three feet tall and entire leaves, all covered with a white woolly down; the flowers, white, come in slender panicles about one foot long. A clump stands out conspicuously in a border of vividly coloured flowers.

These *Artemisias* prosper in any ordinary soil and are usually increased by division.

Arum (from *aron*, the ancient Greek name of the plant). *A. maculatum* (spotted or blotched; the leaves and spathe, or flower, are often spotted purple). It is the Cuckoo Pint of our woods; two other names for it are Wake Robin and Lords and Ladies. The Arum-lily-like leaves are an attractive glossy green; the spathe is whitish within, usually spotted with purple and the spadix is purple. The Cuckoo Pint shoots up in moist, shady places in early spring and would be ornamental in the semi-wild-garden; but one would have to get it from the woods or the hedges, for it is not obtainable from nurseries.

It gives a delightful foliage effect in the rockery, massed against a grey boulder in a shady spot.

A. conophalloides (cone-shaped spadix), a native of Persia, is more decorative, with its large yellowish green spathe, spotted with purple; but I have not seen it listed in any of our catalogues.

Arundinaria (from *arundo*, reed or cane) comprises some of the most ornamental of the hardy Bamboos, which are best grown in woodland- or water-gardens. Several species are mentioned in *Chapter V,* which deals with foliage plants in the water-garden.

The following two species I saw recently in gardens in the South of England. *A. auricoma* (having golden hairs). The leaves are downy beneath and beautifully variegated above with golden-yellow. The largest are about six inches long and one inch wide. Its stems, seldom more than three feet high, are not much thicker than a knitting-needle and come in grass-like tufts. It is its lovely yellow colouring which makes it such a valuable ornamental in our gardens; some of the leaves are wholly yellow. The very slender stems are a dark purple-green.

The species, a native of Japan, was introduced in 1870.

A. falcata (sickle-shaped; referring to the hooked shape of the racemes). It is not hardy enough for gardens around London, but prospers in Cornwall and other districts enjoying a mild climate. It is beautiful enough for a cold greenhouse where room can be found for it; and it could be grown in a large tub or in a cement box, as some of the more vigorous spreading kinds are out of doors. (This method controls them effectually.) *A. falcata*, a native of the Himalayas, where it is found growing up to altitudes of 7000 feet, attains a height of from ten to fifteen feet in favourable districts. Its stems, tufted, are slender (one and a half inches wide) and glaucous when young. The leaves, three to six inches long, a quarter to an inch wide, are a pleasing shade of pale green and slightly glaucous beneath.

When fully grown into a large clump, it is one of the most graceful of all the Bamboos. Like the other species, it needs a deep, rich moist soil and is easily propagated by dividing up the roots.

Arundo (an old Latin name for *Arundo donax*). A genus of about six species of tall, reed-like, ornamental Grasses with plumose, terminal panicles usually white or a shade of pink. They are unfortunately tender. *A. donax* is the hardiest but this species succeeds only in sheltered gardens and, like the Bamboo just described, is often grown in a conservatory.

In the south one sometimes comes across it growing on the banks of a stream or a pond, which is the best place for it as it gets there all the moisture it needs. It will then reach a height of twelve feet or more (in California specimens twenty feet tall are common), the stout stems shooting up from a strong, knotty root-stock. The narrow, rush-like leaves (one to two feet long, about two inches wide) are a greyish green and very striking in the regularity of their arrangement up the stems. The plumes, the largest two feet long, are first a reddish pink, then they turn white. Unlike most of the Bamboos, this plant does not spread rapidly.

The variety *variegata*, whose leaves are striped with white, is smaller and less hardy than the type.

Aspidistra. Everybody knows it, but few people grow it nowadays; and nobody seems to know where all the plants our parents and grandparents grew came from. Apparently they weren't supplied by nurseries. (I have been told by an old inhabitant of Marlow, that it was always possible

110

to get them at the weekly markets, from vendors of pots and chinaware.)

A. lurida is the specific name of the plant. It will tolerate almost everything except frost. Dust, drought, cold draughts do not harm it. It has been knocked off side-boards and tables and thrown in on top of a load of furniture in a removal-van, and survived.

It is a native of China and in warm climates is grown outside in borders. In Florida it is planted in sunny positions along the banks of streams and provides a magnificent show of green luxuriant foliage all the year. The variegated form var. *variegata* is not used, however, as in rich moist soil it speedily loses its green and white stripes. It is best grown as a pot-plant in light sandy compost.

In some countries the Aspidistra is widely cultivated in cool greenhouses for its handsome evergreen leaves, which are cut off by the hundred and sold to florists, who use them as a foil to exotic flowers like the lovely pink *Lilium japonicum*.

I have only once seen it planted out in English gardens: by the side of a pool where it looked as handsome as any other foliage plant I could name. Transplanting it, and giving it a cool rich soil had a beneficial effect on the plant, and it grew more strongly and its foliage improved when it was potted up for the winter.

The variegated form with its alternate green and white stripes is an excellent foliage plant for setting in the middle of a large round formal bed. Plant round it low-growing multi-coloured Carpet-bedders.

In a pot *A. lurida* needs a compost of rich leafy loam and sand and plenty of water (although it has been known to live for weeks without any). Propagate it by root-division in early spring.

Aspidistra is from *aspidiseon*, a small round shield, which refers probably to the shape of the stigma; and the specific epithet, meaning lurid, dingy yellow or brown, no doubt refers to the lurid purple flowers.

Aubrietia deltoidea(deltoid, triangular-shaped: the leaves are usually wedge-shaped). This is the famous plant which has produced so many well-known garden forms. Several have variegated foliage, which is bright all through the autumn and winter; the flowers are much less striking though than those of the best kinds. *A. deltiodea aurea* and *A. d. aurea variegata* have golden-yellow leaves, which make a charming edging to a border, or provide a sunny golden mass of foliage among rocks. The flowers of *A. d. aurea variagata*, which is used as an edging plant in the Oxford Botanical Garden, are a washy lavender shade and very small.

The genus was named in honour of Claude Aurbriet, 1668—1743, the eminent French botanical artist.

Avena sterilis is an ornamental Grass which we usually raise from seed, sowing it in the spring out of doors where the plant is to grow. It is about two feet tall and graceful with its loose, drooping panicles. Its common name is Animated Oats; it is so called because of the quivering movement of the awns, caused by atmospheric changes.

Bambusa. Some of the finest species we grow are described under *Arundinaria* and Phyllostachys in *Chapter V.*

Begonia (to commemorate Michael Begon, 1638—1710, a well-known patron of botany in France).

B. rex (king, ruler). The finest of all the foliage Begonias we cultivate; a native of Assam, India; and the chief progenitor of numerous magnificent foliage varieties. All of them must be housed during the winter in this country; but they give gorgeous pattern-effects in shady borders out of doors during the summer. They deserve to be more widely used.

The original plant has a thick fleshy rhizome; leaves eight to twelve inches long, six to eight inches wide, heart-shaped at the base, very hairy and toothed. They are of a rich metallic green and have a zone of silver-grey running parallel with the margin. The long stalks are reddish and hairy. The small rose-coloured flowers come freely in the summer but are eclipsed by the beauty of the leaves.

Bergenia ligulata (ligulate, strap-shaped). A well-known plant with several specific names. It is often referred to as a Saxifrage (*Saxifraga ligulata*); *Megasea* is another generic name. (The genus *Bergenia* was named in honour of Karl August Bergen, 1704—60, a botanist of Frankfurt.) The species is prized as a foliage plant, the large heart-shaped leaves spreading out and touching the ground as do those of the Hosta, though those of the Bergenia are not so numerous. In warm sheltered gardens they remain during the winter and are then a good foil to the long flower-spikes of rose-coloured flowers, which in the south come into bloom in February. I grow it in front of the evergreen Barberry *Mahonia aquifolium*, which sometimes blooms (yellow flowers) at the same time; the two together making a fine edging group to a lawn. The *Bergenia* will be damaged by severe frost in exposed places and it is therefore wise to give it some protection. Planted on its own at the foot of a shady boulder in a rockery it makes an imposing feature. It needs a good loamy soil and is increased by division.

Those who are particularly fond of its flowers have forced it into bloom by Christmas. It is a native of Nepal, Northern India.

Beta (from *bett*, the Celtic word for red). The edible Beet we grow in our gardens has bronzy purple ovalish leaves and is occasionally used in formal bedding schemes — and with charming effect, especially when accompanied by deep crimson dwarf flowers.

There are several kinds with ornamental foliage, viz. 'Dell's Black-leaved', with long narrow bronze-red leaves; 'Brazilian Beet', with fleshy green leaves which have yellow or crimson veins; these are two of the most striking, and excellent foliage plants for growing in a group at the front of the herbaceous border.

They like a deeply dug, rather light loam and full sun; seed should be sown in early May where they are to grow.

I have used *Beta* var. *cruenta* (blood-coloured) as an edging to a round bed of Sweet William var. *nigrescens*. This Beet has large, showy red leaves with yellow mid-ribs; and the Sweet William is the famous black-crimson-flowered variety with deep purple foliage.

Blechnum tabulare (almost flat like a board). The generic name is from *blechnon*, the Greek name of a Fern. A species found wild in the West Indies, South Africa and other hot regions and usually grown in a conservatory. Its tough, wiry-looking fronds belie its true nature; around London it is best housed during the winter months.

Watering from above will turn its fronds black; potted plants should be stood in a receptacle containing water till they have absorbed sufficient to thoroughly moisten the soil. This should be a mixture of two parts leaf mould, one part loam and one part coarse sand. Those who can grow it out in the open, should water it by placing the rose of the watering-can below the leaves.

The stem on a well-grown specimen is strong, woody and erect, from one to two feet high; the lovely, bronze-green leaves, pinnate, are up to two feet long and eight inches wide.

B. spicant is our native Hard Fern, which occurs in most counties. It grows in moist shady places as a rule and is said by collectors not to be rare. It is no less easy to establish in gardens than its exotic relative. Bailey says it needs "deepest shade". The fronds are about twelve inches long and two inches wide and of a deep green colour. The plant needs a lime-free soil and does as well in clay as in peat.

Brassica (an old Latin name of the Cabbage). Tall specimens, seven or eight feet, with purplish green curly leaves, may be seen in the foliage borders at University Botanic Garden, Oxford. They could be used as back-row plants in the herbaceous border or for massing on the bank of a stream. I like to see them and I think they should be more widely grown.

Butomus umbellatus (arranged in umbels; referring to the flowers). Our native Water Rush, and found wild in many temperate parts of the world. "Lovely deep pink. For bog or shallow water" is the description in Hillier's catalogue. The rose-coloured flowers come in loose umbels in summer; the leaves, bronzy when young, then green, are from two to three feet long. An ornamental Rush for the water-garden. Propagation: by division of the root-stock in spring.

Butomus is from the Greek *bous*, ox; and *temno*, to cut; the sharp leaves will lacerate the mouths of cattle that feed upon them.

Caladium bicolor. Like the exotic *Begonia rex*, the Caladium is seldom grown out of doors in this country. L. H. Bailey in *The Standard Cyclopedia of Horticulture* describes the Caladium as: "Warmhouse, large-leaved plants, grown for the foliage; also employed in summer bedding". I have only once seen a variety of the above species planted in a formal bed. The leaves, shaped like those of our wild Arum, were pale green, translucent and beautifully marked with crimson and pink. The pink colouring shone through the leaves and was very conspicuous in sunlight. Too delicate a plant for most gardens (it needs a hothouse temperature in winter) but vies in the beauty of its foliage with the Begonia.

Canna. These plants are well known to most

people. They see them in formal beds, usually in the gardens of seaside resorts; they seem to do best within reach of the warm sea air. During the winter the tubers are lifted and kept in a frost-proof greenhouse. Store them in moist soil or in leaves.

Garden forms of the Gladiolus-flowered section are preferred by gardeners; these have large brilliantly coloured flowers. But the long sheath-like leaves, often a glaucous-green, as in 'Lutetia', are attractive for many months of the year.

Cannas are favourite plants for sub-tropical effects and need a rich loamy soil and generous feeding with weak liquid manure through the growing season.

Species such as *C. warszewiczii* are less frequently grown nowadays, but this particular one has very handsome leaves. It is figured in the *Botanical Magazine*, Vol. 81 (1855). "This fine Canna was introduced into German gardens in 1849 by M. von Warszewicz from Costa Rica; it is now very generally cultivated in England and is well deserving of it. . . . The leaves are about one foot long and in the widest part about six inches across; they are ovate or ovate-oblong, gradually tapering, and terminating in an almost thread-like apex; they are of a dark green, the mid-rib and veins below being more or less intensely red, as is also their margin."

Cannabis sativa (sown, not spontaneous). One considers it rather apprehensively, for it is the plant from which the toxic Hashish is made. On the other hand it sounds harmless enough when one reads that its seeds are used in bird-seed mixture.

Its finger-shaped leaves (with five to seven narrow leaflets) greyish green in colour, are its chief attraction, the flowers being greenish and insignificant. It is quite a giant and will go up to a height of eight or ten feet. A handsome tall foliage plant for the back of a border, and useful for sub-tropical bedding. Ordinary garden soil suits this foliage annual, which is raised from seed sown in spring.

Cassinia fulvida (fulvous; deep yellow or reddish yellow). No doubt the epithet refers to the golden-yellow colour of the undersides of the leaves, which is always most pronounced in early spring, when new growth commences.

The plant is known as the Golden Heath of New Zealand, where it grows wild often at altitudes of 3500 feet. The species is an evergreen shrub, about four feet tall in this country and apparently not completely hardy everywhere. It survives most frosts, however, in gardens around London. Its flowers are quite ugly: they come in small hanging clusters and are a dirty white colour. The tiny leaves, about a quarter of an inch long and half as wide, are dark green above and golden-yellow beneath.

This is a good shrubby plant for a prominent place. Set it in the front of a flower border; don't attempt to prune it into shape but let it grow freely, and cut off the flower-heads as soon as they begin to show.

Cassinia fulvida likes a peaty, loamy soil and is easily increased by cuttings, which will root out of doors in shady sheltered places.

Small specimens (nine inches tall) planted in association with slips of the silver Lavender Cotton are singularly charming as an edging: the golden foliage behind, the silver in front. The generic name honours Count Cassini, a French botanist who died in 1832.

Celmisia coriacea (tough and leathery). A perennial also from New Zealand and prized both for its daisy-like white or yellow flowers and its narrow, lanceolate leathery leaves, eight to

121

twenty-four inches long, which are covered with a delicate whitish skin above and silvery down beneath. The leaves form a spreading rosette and, with the long, mealy flower-stalks, make a charming foliage-plant before the flowers appear. It is most striking, perhaps, when it is seen against grey rock-work. A light well-drained soil and a sunny position are required. The plant does best in warm sheltered places.

C. gracilenta (slender, thin). The species is offered by Hillier, whose catalogue describes it as having "grassy leaves and white daisy flowers in summer". It is a dwarf (from New Zealand); the slender leaves an eighth of an inch wide are from three to twelve inches long and covered with a white cobwebby substance. An ideal plant for a sunny spot in the rockery. A well-drained soil is necessary. Both plants are best increased by cuttings, or good-sized specimens can be divided up.

Centaurea rutifolia often appears in catalogues under *C. cineraria* (Dusty Miller). Its fern-like leaves, silvery white and downy, are much valued for formal beds, its pale purplish flowers being pinched out before they have a chance to develop. It goes up to a height of three feet if left unpruned, but many gardeners cut it back judiciously to keep it low and bushy. The species, a native of Italy, likes an open loamy soil, plenty of sun and is grown from seed and from cuttings. Although listed as a hardy perennial in catalogues, it has been known to succumb to frost and prolonged spells of wet weather.

Hillier includes *C. simplicicaulis*, which is suitable for rockeries. It has small, finely cut leaves, silvery white and downy and pink flowers which come in June. The species, a native of Armenia, needs a gritty loam, and is a good plant for the scree.

Cerastium tomentosum. For a display of soft silvery white foliage, there are few alpines to rival it; but it is a notorious spreader, creeping far by means of its underground stems. And once it establishes itself it is extremely difficult to eradicate. It has been recommended for formal beds; but if it is used (I never use it in bedding out) it should be planted only along edgings. It is not suitable for a rockery, for it would soon smother any alpines growing near it. Yet its foliage is attractive enough to make one want to possess the plant. The best and the safest place for it is on a sunny arid slope where little else will grow.

In thin sandy soil, its leaves, small and oblong-shaped, take on an even whiter colour. The flowers are pure white and come on stems six inches tall.

Cerastium is from *keras*, meaning horn; the seed of many of the species is horn-shaped.

Cnicus benedictus is the Blessed Thistle, a hardy annual, with arching Fern-like leaves marked with silvery white. It grows two feet tall and has small pale yellow flower-heads in summer. It is easily raised from seed and makes a decorative silver-foliage plant for the flower-border.

Coleus are tender plants noted for the vivid colouring of their leaves. As they withstand shearing, they are chosen by gardeners for Carpet-bedding; varieties like the old "Golden Bedder", appearing in many of the intricate designs we see in public gardens. *C. blumei*, which is thought to be of hybrid origin, has produced many garden forms with variously-coloured leaves. They are deeply and coarsely toothed and ovalish in shape. (*See page 58.*) *Coleus blumei* is beautifully illustrated in the *Botanical Magazine*, Vol. 79 (1853) In the description of the plant the author says

"We are indebted for our first knowledge of this plant in a living state to Mr. Law, of Clapton Nursery, who received the plant from Belgium, as a native of Java; but even there, Blume speaks of it only as cultivated in gardens. As such it is an extremely ornamental plant, the leaves being intensely mottled and blotched with deep purple or sanguinous stains, while the long whorled racemes of flowers are prettily varied with purple and white. Nothing is more easily cultivated, and no stove should be without it, for it flowers through the summer, and till the setting-in of the winter."

Cortaderia argentea (silvery). The silvery white plumes are well known, though perhaps now this plant, the Pampas Grass, is not so widely grown. Dividing it up, or even digging and weeding near it can be hazardous, the long narrow rush-like leaves having razor-sharp edges.

In time it makes an enormous, rather untidy clump with tall, bending canes or stems which carry the plumose panicles, these sometimes being tinged with pink. They are the chief feature of the plant during the autumn: sometimes left, sometimes cut and brought indoors for winter decoration. Cut them before they are fully open, otherwise the spikelets will immediately begin to drop.

In the past, the Pampas Grass seems to have appealed to owners of quite small gardens. But it is not adapted for limited spaces and is never seen to best advantage on small lawns or in narrow borders.

It needs deep loamy or sandy soil and a position sheltered from winds, which damage the plumes.

There are several varieties; catalogues list at least two, viz. var. *pumila*, a dwarf compact form, four feet high, with shorter plumes; and var. *rendatleri* which has reddish pink plumes.

The big type plant is usually grown in the centre of a large lawn. I can't think of a more suitable place for it.

This handsome giant Rush-grass is a native of temperate South America. *Cortadero* is the Argentine name for Pampas Grass.

Cyclamen neapolitanum (of the district of Naples). It is found wild in Southern Europe, from France as far south as Greece. The rose-pink flowers come in late summer or autumn before the leaves and resemble in colour and shape the much larger ones of the common greenhouse variety we grow in pots, *C. persica*.

The leaves of our plant are small, roundish and marbled and fully developed by late autumn. For several months of the year they provide beautiful mat-like patches of foliage in semi-shady places. This species is an inhabitant of woodlands (it has been naturalised in Britain) and is perhaps the loveliest of all the autumn plants we can grow in semi-wild places. It is excellent for the rockery, too, where it must have a well-drained soil, which, as in the shady woodland, should be enriched by an annual dressing of bone-meal in early spring.

The corms, large and flat, are covered with about an inch of soil when they are planted. On heavy soil, work in some lime-rubble round them; this keeps it open and porous. A good compost consists of two parts loam, one part sifted leaf mould and one part coarse sand.

Seed is produced in abundance and, as soon as it forms, it should be gathered and sown in a warm protected place out of doors.

Cyclamen is from the Greek *kyklos*, circular, the peduncles (flower-stalks) coil round when in seed.

There is a fine show of this Cyclamen at the

Savill Gardens.

Corms are obtainable from most bulb specialists.

Cynara scolymus (Greek name of a Thistle-like plant). This is the Globe Artichoke, which is grown in many kitchen-gardens for the delicious vegetable produced by the flower-heads. (The scales or involucre bracts are the parts eaten — cooked in boiling salt water and served with melted butter.) But the plant also has its aesthetic value. It is a magnificent silver thistle with large Fern-like leaves somewhat spiny and covered with a white downy substance beneath.

The plant will attain a height of six feet in good rich open loam and in a sheltered warm place. But even when half that size (which it often is), it is a fine ornamental for the herbaceous border. I like to see it grown well to the front and in company with other silvery-leaved things such as the Lavender Cotton and the white-leaved Artemisias. The flowers are purple and very large.

It can be increased by suckers, the shoots being detached from the crown in spring and planted out in a sheltered bed.

The Globe Artichoke has never been found

Aspidistra variegata

Verbascum olympicum

Caladium

Sedum acre

Tulipa greigii, hybrids

Gymnocarpa

Hart's Tongue

wild and is probably derived from the Cardoon of Southern Europe. (*C. cardunculus*).

The generic name is from *kynos*, dog; the spines of the involucre have been likened to a dog's teeth.

Cyperus longus (long, tall) is a hardy ornamental Grass and listed in many nurserymen's catalogues. It will be found growing by the side of our streams and ditches and is easily established in the water-garden. The stems carrying the branched panicles (reddish brown) are from two to four feet tall; the leaves, Grass-like, a bright shining green above and paler beneath.

It is best increased by division.

Cyperus is an ancient Greek name of the plant; *Cyperum* is quoted by Pliny: "a kind of rush".

Dahlia (named in honour of Professor Andreas Dahl, a Swedish botanist and a pupil of Linnaeus). There are several species, natives of Mexico, which were introduced into Spain during the eighteenth and nineteenth centuries. Our popular garden Dahlias are clonal varieties derived from some of these. They give a magnificent display of brilliantly coloured flowers, and one 'Bishop of Llandaff', a Paeony-flowered type, with crimson-scarlet flowers, has rich

129

purplish foliage, which is often used with magnificent effect in formal bedding schemes. The plant takes up much room and can be used only in large beds. An arrangement in which a group of this Dahlia is surrounded by red-leaved Beets and bright blue Lobelia is popular with many gardeners. Dahlias want a rich soil; the tubers should be lifted at the end of the summer and stored in frost-proof sheds.

Dianthus, like the Dahlias, are chiefly grown for their flowers and most of them have the additional charm of fragrance. The slender leaves of many species and garden forms are a delightful blue-grey colour and attractive all through the year. They show up to best advantage, I think, when seen against the dark green grassy rufts of the *Armeria*.

The Cheddar Pink, *D. gratianopolitanus* (of the district of Grenoble) often appears in catalogues as *D. caesius*. It is the most popular of the species and has pretty blue-grey foliage. Use it as an edging to the flower-borders, or let it form a spreading mat-like clump at the foot of a rock. Its spiky bluish foliage stands out well against grey stone-work, especially through the winter. It is a native of Europe and found wild in some parts of Britain.

The garden Pinks are special favourites. 'Mrs Sinkins', with very fragrant white flowers and blue-grey foliage, is one of the oldest and among the best of edging-plants. So are the dwarfer Allwoodii alpine kinds such as 'Wink' and 'Tinker-bell'. These can be used for massing in a pocket in the rockery.

D. barbatas (bearded, with tufts of long hair). This is the Sweet William. From the plant our popular fragrant garden varieties are derived. It is of little value as a foliage plant, but the variety *nigrescens*, with dark crimson flowers and deep copper-coloured leaves, is often used as an ornamental bedder, like the red-leaved Dahlia.

Dianthus need a light sandy loamy soil and full sun. They are increased by cuttings or by dividing up the plants. The Sweet William is easily raised from seed.

Dryopteris (from *dryad*, a wood-nymph; and *pteris*, Fern). A large genus of Ferns: over 1200 species are recognised. Several are natives of Britain; and many are cultivated in our gardens. On the whole, though, it is difficult to find an appropriate place for them in the average small garden. They look best in woodland or among rocks.

The following are some of the most ornamental and have proved highly successful under cultivation.

D. erythrosora (red sori: the sori, or spore-cases, on the under-surface of Fern-leaves). A hardy Fern from Japan and China, with decorative fronds eighteen inches long and half as wide, which are dark green above and red or red-brown beneath. I have come across it in London gardens, growing against shady walls; it is deciduous there, dying right back in the winter. In a cool greenhouse its foliage is evergreen.

D. filix-mas (Male Fern). It likes a shady moist situation and a lightish peaty soil. The largest fronds measure three feet in length by twelve inches wide. It is found in many parts of the world, including Britain. Nurseries offer various different forms of this species: var. *Barnesii*, of erect habit and with spear-shaped fronds; var. *Bollandiae*, a plumose variety, with very finely cut fronds.

D. spinulosa (having small spines) is another native species and likes plenty of moisture at its roots all through the year. A shady spot near water suits it admirably. I have grown it

132

successfully on the edge of a pool. The leaves, a fresh green colour, are about twelve inches long and half as wide. The variety *intermedia*, with bigger fronds, is common in the woods of the Northern States of America and much valued for cutting.

Epimedium. These plants are by no means common. The following are grown in shady places among rocks in the Savill Gardens, Windsor.

E. pinnatum (pinnatifid: divided into lobes). The leaves are rather like those of a large Maidenhair-fern. The leaflets, ovalish heart-shaped, are delicate-looking and tinged with bronze in April. The flowers, small and yellow, come on long slender stems about twelve inches long. *Habitat*: Persia.

E. × *rubrun* (red). The plant is thought to be a hybrid between *E. alpinum* and *E. grandiflorum*. With its small leaflets, touched with red in early spring, this is one of the loveliest of foliage plants for edging a woodland garden. The tiny flowers are yellow and less decorative than the leaves.

E. ×*versicolor* (changeable in colour). The plant at Windsor grows in woodland. The leaflets, longish heart-shaped, are heavily splashed with bronze-red and then turn pale green. The tall sprays of flowers, greenish yellow, do not last long.

Epimediums are choice plants for shady places and revel in a light sandy leafy soil. They are increased by root-division in August.

Euphorbia. Many of these plants have attractive glaucous leaves and greenish yellow flowers, which from a distance have the appearance of small, fresh, young leaf-growths. There is a fine collection at Oxford. The following will be found in the different foliage borders. They do well in practically any soil — even the poorest — and like full sun.

E. characias (Latin name of 'Wolf's Milk', *E. helioscopia*, our native Spurge). This is the handsomest and most imposing of them all; its thick stems go up to a height of six feet and have regularly spaced, narrow strap-shaped leaves; at the top the inflorescence stem shoots up and carries greenish flowers with a brown centre. The stems, when broken, exude a white milky substance.

E. epithymoides is quite a dwarf, with stems twelve inches long forming a clump which is covered with yellow greenish flowers in April. The small narrow oblong leaves are a dark blue-green.

E. gregersenii is another small species with narrow leaves and green-yellow rosette-flowers.

E. sikkimensis, taller, has reddish pink stems and narrow, very striking pink-veined leaves.

E. wulfenii resembles *E. characias*, except that it is not quite so tall. It makes a similarly imposing shrubby clump, however; the leaves, narrow and bluish green, are densely carried on the stems; the flowers, round and green, have yellow bracts. Bean describes the plant in *Trees and Shrubs Hardy in the British Isles*: "Native of Dalmatia; introduced some time previous to 1837, in which year it flowered in the Horticultural Society's Garden at Chiswick. The inflorescence opens in spring and remains in good colour for two or three months."

The green-yellow flowers of the *Euphorbia* soon pall on one, and a border full of the plants (as at Oxford) is not particularly attractive. But as foil-plants (or buffer-plants between groups of perennials) they are admirable. A place should be found in every border for the tall *E. characias*. I grow it in association with a large-leaved Hosta

135

—both placed well to the front of a flower-border.

Euphorbias are best divided up every third year.

Ferns. These foliage plants are less often grown in gardens nowadays. Gardens being smaller, the plants are perhaps little considered. Most of them need special sites: shady spots in the woodland or damp places, say, at the foot of a rock. Shady town gardens, surrounded by walls, often provide suitable sites for some, however. The different kinds described in this list will be found under the following genera: *Blechnum*; *Dryopteris*; *Onoclea*; *Osmunda*; *polypodium*.

Festuca ovina glauca. The Sheep's Fescue; the charming glaucous-blue grass which is variously used in gardens. It is good for edging or for massing in a large group at the front of the herbaceous border; and as a groundwork to certain flowering-plants it is delightful. Plant it among the heavily fragrant white and purple Regale Lilies. Every third year it will be wise to lift some of the tufts and divide them up to prevent them from encroaching on the Lily clumps. The *Festuca* grows about nine inches high, the panicles of white-cream spikelets come on stems rather taller.

The plant likes a light leafy soil on the moist side.

Festuca in Latin is 'stalk, stem, straw'.

Gunnera (to commemorate the Norwegian bishop and botanist T. Ernst Gunner, 1718—73). Some species have the largest leaves of any plant we grow in these Islands (nine feet or more across in warm sheltered gardens), while others have leaves only an inch or two long.

Gunnera are usually grown in moist boggy places: by the waterside or in water-gardens; they like sun but dislike wind; it often tears their enormous leaves and damages them irreparably.

The first listed here, however, does well in drier soils — for instance, in borders.

G. chilensis (from Chile) has leaves four to five feet across on stems three to six feet long. The leaves, lobed and deeply toothed, are less spiny than those of the better-known species, *G. manicata*. The flowers are red and come in long panicles.

G. magellanica (from the district of Magellan, South America). This is one of the miniatures; it has leaves not more than two and a half inches wide, which spread out on the creeping stems, forming a pleasing mat of dark green foliage.

An ideal plant for the rockery or a small water-garden. To get it to grow successfully, it must never lack water.

G. manicata (having a dense hairy covering that can be stripped off). This the largest species, with leaves sometimes eight feet or so across on thick prickly stems — most striking in April before the leaves have developed. It may be seen at Kew on the banks of the lake, in company with the waterside Saxifrage *Peltiphyllum peltatum*, which has leaves about one foot wide.

Some gardeners who grow the plant leave the flower-panicles to develop; but if they are cut off the leaves grow larger. This species, a native of Brazil, was introduced in 1867.

Around London the large-leaved Gunneras need protection through the winter months; and usually the dead leaves and dried Bracken are piled up over them till late spring.

Hedera is the genus of Ivies, which are mostly used as climbers on walls; but the shrub- or tree-Ivies, as they are called, make excellent foliage plants for borders and shrubberies. At Oxford the variety of the Common Ivy, *H. helix conglomerata* (clustered), with small leaves, stands out conspicuously in one of the foliage borders. The erect, stiff stems are from eighteen inches to two feet high; they are branched and crowded with small greyish-green leaves. It is a rather difficult type of plant to accommodate in the garden. I have seen it grown in a pot and stood on a paved walk.

The Persian Ivy, *H. colchica*, may be similarly grown. Bean says: "The tree form makes a striking evergreen bush with uniformly ovate leaves". The entire or slightly lobed leaves (three to seven inches wide) are more attractive in the variety *H. colchica dentata variegata*, these being blotched with gold. I have seen it grown as a background to deep blue Delphiniums.

Hedera is an ancient Latin name of the Ivy; and *helix* is Greek for a twining plant.

Helxine soleirolii was named in honour of Lieut. Soleirol (b. 1792), who collected it in Corsica.

There is only one species and it is fairly common in our gardens. It forms a pleasing mat of Cress-like, bright green leaves and in shade creeps rapidly over the ground: over stones, soil or grass and up shady walls. Frost often turns it black, but the plant recovers quickly and in most shady places can be something of a pest. In an

Alpine Lawn it would smother things growing near it and is best relegated to a place among shady damp rocks where little else will grow, or to a piece of ground on the north side of the house. It is easily increased by cuttings.

Hemerocallis (from the Greek *hemera*, a day; *kallos*, beauty). This is the Day Lily, which has long, narrow rush-like leaves, especially decorative in spring and autumn; the flowers, ephemeral, coming successionally through June and July.

Most catalogues list several species and varieties. One of the best is *H. aurantiaca* var. *major*. The flowers are of an orange-yellow shade, funnel-shaped, about five inches across; the leaves three feet long and one inch wide.

H. fulva (fulvous, tawny) has reddish copper flowers and leaves three feet long. Several varieties such as the double-flowered var. *flore pleno* and var. *cypriana*, with bright glossy green leaves, are in cultivation.

Hemerocallis prosper in any ordinary soil and are increased by division of the clumps. The plants are mostly grown in the herbaceous border, their leaves providing an agreeable contrast with the more ordinary round or oblong shapes.

These Day Lilies are also grown in semi-wild-gardens and are well adapted for growing on the banks of a stream or a pool.

Heracleum mantegazzianum (named in honour of Paola Mantegazzi (1831—1910), Italian anthropologist). A giant Cow Parsley; its other name is the Cartwheel Flower. The plant is twice as big as a man and can only be used, I think, in the wild-garden or woodland — it would be all right with Bamboos on the side of a large pool. The thick stems are topped with large white flowers which come in flattish umbels, the biggest four feet in diameter. But the deeply divided leaves, three feet long, are its great attraction. It needs a rich moist soil to attain really giant proportions and there are very few gardens that can accommodate it. Seedlings shoot up all over the place where the plant grows; to avoid this nuisance, cut the flower-heads off as they begin to fade.

Hillier offers the species *H. villosum*, whose leaves are woolly tomentose beneath. It is as large as the other species; both are natives of the Caucasus.

Holcus lanatus albo-variegatus (woolly, white variegated; the generic name is from the old

Greek word *holkos*, a grass). A little tufted orna-mental Grass, striped silver and green. It is excellent for edging, though it runs rather freely and should not be allowed to spread among perennials. It would perhaps be less troublesome in the rockery and, set against the weathered surface of stone, its woolly silvery green foliage shows up to perfection. Sandy soil suits it; and it is easily propagated by division.

Hosta (named in honour of Nicholas Thomas Host, 1761—1834, a Viennese physician). The plants are often referred to as *Funkia* and some-times listed in catalogues under that name. They are known as Plaintain Lilies and erroneously as Day Lilies. The tubular flowers, white to dark lavender, are not striking and they don't last long — though longer than a day. The plants are grown specifically for their beautifully shaped cool-looking leaves. The dense stools or clumps of foliage show up to best advantage at the edge of a border, where some of the leaves spread out across the path and incidentally provide a pleasing break in a long straight line. A deep rich soil is best (one part loam and one part leaf mould); and partial shade suits them better than full sun.

An ideal setting for them is the water-garden: grow them on the margin of a pool or along the bank of a stream.

H. fortunei (to commemorate Robert Fortune, 1812—80, the famous plant collector). A native of Japan, with grey-green leaves, not large, about eight inches by six inches wide, and not so glaucous as those of *H. glauca*. The var. *marginato-alba* has leaves which are margined with white. This Hosta in particular gives a superbly beautiful effect when it is massed in a woodland clearing.

H. glauca, with glaucous-blue-green leaves, twelve inches long and about nine inches across, is widely grown in gardens and much admired for its delightful green and the beautiful veining of the leaves. (The conspicuous veining in the Hostas is one of their great charms.) A native of Japan. Introduced in 1830. The plant is usually listed in catalogues under *Funkia sieboldiana*.

H. lancifolia (lance-shaped, tapering to both ends). This small-leaved species (also from Japan) is a good choice for the rockery, its green leaves, five inches long and half as wide, looking doubly cool and attractive near a small pool. The var. *albo-marginata* has white-margined leaves.

H. plantaginea (Plaintain-like) has fragrant white flowers in August or September and ovalish heart-shaped, conspicuously veined leaves. It is said to be less hardy than the others and does best against a shady wall.

H. sieboldiana (named for P. F. von Siebold, 1796—1866, Dutch collector of plants in Japan). The species is figured in the *Botanical Magazine*, Vol. 65 (1839), and was thought at that time to be tender. "The present plant is a species belonging to that Genus (Funkia), for a knowledge of which we are indebted to Dr. Siebold, the celebrated Japanese Traveller, who found it in Japan, and introduced it to the gardens of Belgium, whence it was received by Mr. Murray at the Glasgow Botanic Gardens from Mr. M'coy. It flowers in the greenhouse in July."

H. undulata (wavy). The rich green leaves, waved, and blotched with white, are six inches long and half as wide; they come on stalks rather longer. The plant has pale bluish flowers which bloom in August.

These handsome foliage plants may be obtained from any nursery specialising in herbaceous material. They improve through the course of the years and should not be disturbed once a suitable place has been found for them. It is possible to increase one's stock by cutting off some of the pieces with roots attached from the outside of large mature specimens.

Hypericum × *moserianum* var. *tricolor*. Most of the St. John's Worts are grown for their bright yellow flowers; the popular one being the creeping, insidious Rose of Sharon(*H. calycinum*).

Our plant is the variegated form of the hybrid raised by Moser, of France, from *H. patulum* and *H. calycinum* — its common name is the Gold Flower.

Var. *tricolor* is grown in foliage-borders for its leaves, small, narrow and beautifully coloured green, red and yellow. The red, often a deep carmine shade, is particularly striking and shows up conspicuously in early spring before the smallish flowers (two inches across) appear. It is said to be less hardy than the other; but it does well in the Oxford Botanic Garden.

Grow it in a fairly light leafy soil in a sunny place. You can raise new plants from cuttings taken in late summer.

Iresine (from *eiros*, wool; the stems of the plants are woolly). These are bedders, with vividly coloured leaves and stems; they are, like many other kinds, tender and have to be housed in a warm place all the winter and spring. Not till June is it safe to put them outside.

I. herbstii (in honour of Mr. Herbst, of Kew, who introduced it from the River Platte, U.S.A.) has broadly ovalish leaves, purplish red above and crimson beneath; the stems are a bright carmine and the plant reaches a height of twelve inches or so. The flowers, white or greenish, are insignificant.

Iresine will tolerate clipping; it makes them bushy and keeps them low and neat for Carpet-bedding or ribbon-planting. There are many gorgeously coloured varieties. Var. *wallisii*, with black-purple foliage, is one of the dwarfest. Var. *brilliantissima* is a deep crimson. *I. biemuelleri* is thought to be another variety and is a compact dwarf with crimson stems and leaves.

These bedders must be planted in full sun and may be increased by cuttings set in sandy soil in a hothouse.

Iris (from the Greek word for rainbow). We grow Irises principally for their flowers; unfortunately, they don't last long; but the foliage, decorative on most of the plants and evergreen on some, is interesting for the best part of the year.

One or two are outstanding: *I. foetidissima variegata*, with beautiful glaucous leaves and orange-red berries, is a fine waterside plant. Two others also revel in moist situations, viz. *I. pseudacorus variegata* and *I. sibirica*. The first has long narrow glaucous leaves striped with creamy white; the other, Rush-like leaves which make large clumps till the frosts cut them down in November.

The winter-blooming species *I. unguicularis*, has similarly shaped leaves — long, narrow, a paler shade of green than those of *I. sibirica* and make an attractive clump of tough, grey-green foliage during the winter.

I. pallida dalmatica and its varieties are regarded as the most handsome-leaved plants of the family. They are delightfully glaucous and some are striped with cream, yellow or white.

The dwarf *I. pumila*, whose sword-shaped leaves are about nine inches tall, is one of the best of this type of foliage plant for the rockery. Let it grow into a mass in a pocket or at the foot of a boulder and leave it some years before dividing it up. It likes a gritty, loamy soil.

Juniperus horizontalis is an evergreen creeping shrub noted for its very charming glaucous-green foliage. It spreads far by means of its rooting stems and is an excellent choice for some conspicuous site, say, a slope, where its sweeping foliage is shown off to advantage. The var. Douglasii (known as the Waukegan Juniper) is even more striking, with its glaucous-blue foliage, which turns purple in the autumn. The flowers of these plants are insignificant, but the tiny bluish cones are decorative for many months.

These Junipers are natives of North America and like a light loamy soil.

Kniphofia (named in honour of Professor J. H. Kniphof, 1704-63, of Erfurt). The Red-hot Pokers, which we grow principally for their spikes of red or orange-red flowers. The smaller species are sometimes planted in the herbaceous border, where normally room cannot be found for more than one or two, since they eventually make large clumps. They are much more striking massed (a dozen or so) in a round bed on a lawn. Before they flower, their long strap-shaped leaves, bent over and touching the soil, make a delightful picture of lush green foliage. Equally striking are the plants grouped on a sunny slope leading down to the edge of a pool. They need a light, leafy, loamy soil and protection in cold, exposed gardens. Do not disturb them when they are growing well. Old clumps may be divided up in the spring, the rooted pieces being planted out in moist loam and kept well watered till they are established.

For foliage effects, *K. caulescens* and *K. northiae* are the best. The first has thick rhizomes and glaucous-blue-grey leaves. The stems, four to five feet long, carry reddish flower-spikes, the colour becoming paler later in the year. The specific epithet, caulescent, refers to the thick rhizomes, which grow along the surface of the soil. The other has long thick leaves, four inches wide (of a pale grey-green colour), which bend over, seemingly weighted down by their own mass. The flower-spikes are yellow and red and bloom in July. *K. northiae* was named in honour of the talented painter of flowers, Miss Marianne North, 1830—96. Some of her pictures may be seen in the Gallery at Kew Botanic Gardens.

Most nurseries supply the first plant; Hillier's catalogue describes it: "Flowers buff, changing to pale red. Yucca-like growth". The other species is rather rare. Both are natives of South Africa.

Kochia scoparia trichophila is the Fire Bush or

Summer Cypress, a well-known annual which most of us have raised from seed and planted in a pot or in the flower-border. The delicate feathery foliage, which is a charming pale green at first, turns a deep copper or reddish-purple in the autumn. It makes a good ornamental dwarf bush, two and a half feet high, roundish or oblong and symmetrical — its regular shape perhaps limiting its use. It is well adapted for potting and an excellent plant for bedding schemes. More often than not it will be seen planted in a bed with a groundwork of the small tuberous pink Begonias. Its flowers are small and insignificant.

Seed is sown indoors in a temperature of 50°F; the seedlings being transplanted when they are two inches high to single pots. Set them out of doors at the end of May in leafy, loamy soil, which must not be allowed to become dry.

The generic name commemorates Professor Koch, the German botanist, 1771—1849. *Scoparia*, broom-like (the green form was apparently once used in making brooms); *trichophilia*, strongly hairy.

Lamium maculatum (blotched; referring to the leaves, which are marked with white).

L. album is the white Dead Nettle which often creeps unawares into our gardens. *L. maculatum* has similarly-shaped flowers, only a purplish pink, which bloom in early summer. It is, however, as a foliage plant that it is valued; the variety *L. maculatum aureum* is much more decorative, with its furry golden leaves, and a striking foliage plant for moist, fairly rich soils. Grow it as an edging in the flower-borders.

Lanandula (from the Latin *lava*, to wash; referring to the use of Lavender Water in the bath; the perfume is obtained from the flowers). One of the oldest known of the plants we grow in our gardens and perhaps the most fragrant. *L. spica* (spike-like flowers) is the Common Lavender, the Old English, which comes from districts round the Mediterranean. The whitish downy stems and the pale grey leaves make it a fine foliage plant for the herbaceous border. Through the winter its leaves take on a bluer tinge. For edging a long grass walk there is nothing lovelier. It can be clipped annually into a neat shape; but only a light clipping-over is required.

The var. Munstead Dwarf, with darker flowers, blooms earlier, and its foliage seems to have a more bluish grey tinge to it. Light sandy soil is best for the plants; and they need full sun. They are propagated by cuttings, taken in late summer and rooted out of doors.

Ligularia (from *ligula*, strap; the ray-florets are strap-shaped). A family which provides us with some large-leaved plants, suitable for boggy places and for growing near the side of a stream or a pool.

L. clivorum (of the hills), a native of China; a handsome foliage plant for massing along the banks of a stream. The leaves are from ten to twenty inches wide, roundish and coarsely toothed; their stalks six to twelve inches long. In July and August the orange-yellow flowers come on stems about four feet tall. 'Desdemona' is a striking variety frequently seen nowadays. It has vivid orange Daisy-like blooms, its stems are dark purple as are the undersides of the large cool-looking leaves.

L. veitchiana grows well at the Savill Gardens and is a beautifully formed waterside plant, with its triangular heart-shaped leaves two feet wide, from which rise in summer tall stems carrying golden-yellow Daisy flowers. Cut the stems and the flowers off as soon as the latter fade, and the plant becomes a shapely mound of handsome green leaves.

Ligularia need a rich peaty soil and they are increased by division.

Lunaria annua variegata, the variegated Honesty, an annual or usually a biennial. Its variegated leaves (some are almost wholly white) are more attractive than the purplish flowers. It makes a fine border-plant; and I like to see it beside a bold clump of low-growing Hostas. (Both prefer shady places.) The seed-pods, which form in late summer, are valued for indoor decoration during the winter.

The generic name is from *luna*, the Latin name for moon, and refers to the shape and appearance of the seed-vessels.

Lysichitum (from *lysis*, loosening; *chiton*, a cloak; referring to the spathe, which is shed in late spring).

There are but two species — perhaps the most exotic-looking of all the bog or waterside plants we grow. Their foliage, fresh juicy green, is like that of some giant Spinach.

Both are completely hardy, but *L. americanum*, described in the *Botanical Magazine*, Vol. 130 (1904), under the specific name of *L.*

camtchatcense, apparently was a failure when it first grown outside at Kew.

It flourishes in the Savill Gardens, growing there close to the edge of a slow-running stream. Quoting from the *Botanical Magazine*, C. A. Geyer, who collected specimens on the Coeur d'Alene River, Idaho, states that it grew in deep rich vegetable mould, and that its scarlet fruit was a favourite food of the bear.

The largest leaves are often three feet long and eighteen inches across and shoot up strong after the bright yellow Arum-like flowers or spathes have formed. These do not last long and the foliage remains bright and green till the frosts come.

L. camtschatcense has white flowers (the species is similar to the other) and blooms a little later. Both are suitable only for the largest gardens. They are not so striking together in bloom — white has a rather taming effect on yellow.

Magnolias rank among the best of the flowering shrubs we grow. Their blooms are often goblet-shaped or open like large Water-lilies; and the leaves of the evergreen species such as *M. grandiflora* are as handsome as those of many evergreen Rhododendrons. I single this shrub out because it is mostly grown on walls and there, with its branches trained out laterally, it makes a remarkably fine glossy background for the tallest herbaceous plants we grow.

The untidy-looking branches that grow outward should be cut back in late summer.

The glossy green foliage is particularly cheering all through the grey winter months.

Miscanthus (from *miskos*, stem; *anthos*, flower; referring to the stalked spikelets of the panicles). A genus of ornamental Grasses which grow tall and have attractive plumes: in *M. sinensis* they are about twelve inches long, white tinged with red, and come in early autumn. The leaves, two and a half to three feet long, half an inch wide, are blue-green with a white stripe. This species makes a good-sized clump in time and is a graceful feathery plant for a border.

The varieties are more ornamental: in var. *gracillimus* the leaves are much narrower. Var. *variegatus* has creamy longitudinal stripes (the plant often appears under the name var. *fol. striatis*). And var. *zebrinus*, the most striking, has yellow bars running across the leaves.

Miscanthus are often listed as *Eulalia* in

nurserymen's catalogues and still referred to as such by many gardeners who grow them. They are perfectly hardy and will thrive in a lightish soil that doesn't get too dry. The clumps are best divided up every third or fourth year.

Myriophyllum proserpinacoides is the Parrot's Feather, an aquatic which grows luxuriantly in the warm waters of Brazil and other parts of South America.

In Britain it is often used as an ornamental floating-plant in cool greenhouses. It can be planted in a small artificial pool outside and carefully lifted and planted in an aquarium-case (such as one used for goldfish) for the winter. Its whorls of small, finely divided leaves come crowded on the stems, which grow some six inches out of the water. A charming, graceful water-plant. Its roots must be set firmly in a deposit of fibrous loam in shallow water.

Most catalogues list it under *M. brasilense*, which is now a synonym.

The generic name is from two Greek words meaning myriad-leaved; the specific epithet from *proserp*, to creep or crawl along; referring to the stems.

Nepeta is known to most people as Cat Mint;

and the form grown in gardens (usually a hybrid, viz. *N.* × *fassenii*) has small silver-grey leaves, which, when a dozen plants are grouped in a row, give a pleasing drift of grey before the flowers open. It is perhaps the favourite edging-plant for herbaceous borders.

N. hederacea var. *variegata* is quite different with its heart-shaped or Ivy-shaped leaves one and a half inches across, and deep green and white in the middle. It is a spreading, carpeting-plant, fit only for woodland floors or wild spots in large gardens. It is grown in the Oxford Garden, and in April has tiny lavender-coloured flowers. A fine foliage plant for growing round old tree-trunks. It has several common names, viz. Field Balm, Gill over the Ground, Ground Ivy.

Any ordinary soil suits the Nepeta; and they are propagated by division.

N. hederacea var. *variegata* is a native of Europe and is found wild in different parts of the British Isles.

Nymphaea are the Water-lilies. Many, like the Common White Water-lily (*N. alba*), have deeply heart-shaped leaves, red in the young state. It is on large stretches of still water that these wonderfully decorative leaves are seen to perfection. As a background, the big-leaved Gunneras are often planted on one of the banks leading down to the water.

A good way of planting these aquatics is to set them in boxes of fibrous loam (enriched with old cow-manure) and place them at the bottom of the pool; the water must just cover the crowns at first; then more is added as the plants develop and grow taller.

Onoclea sensibilis grows in shady woodland at the Savill Gardens, the young fronds springing up through the rich leaf soil in April, like Bracken. This fern spreads rapidly and is best kept for the woodland- or wild-garden. Its leaves rise to a height of about four feet, the segments being two to six inches long. The foliage contrasts very agreeably with large-leaved plants like the *Rodgersia*. *Onoelea sensibilis* is among the coarser types of Ferns; the young foliage, however, is often damaged by frost, hence the common name Sensitive Fern.

Osmunda regalis is the Royal Fern, rare in our gardens, probably because suitable places cannot always be found for it. It will grow up tall when planted in rich, moist, peaty loam on the north side of a wall or a boulder. A constant supply of water is essential, if the plant is to prosper and make a good specimen.

The stalks are long, the fronds two to six feet tall, in favourable situations; the colour being a pleasing shade of pale green. It has been grown successfully in the water-garden: not actually in water but near the edge of a shallow stream. In autumn the leaves assume charming tints of yellow and gold.

The generic name is from *Osmunder*, a Scandinavian name for Thor.

Peltiphyllum peltatum (target-shaped, shield-like). The variety *nana* (dwarf) may be seen at the foot of a boulder near water in the rockery at Kew Gardens, its flat roundish leaves, lobed and notched, according well with the grey rocks.

The type plant is known as the Umbrella Plant and grows taller, the leaves, six inches across, coming on stems about two feet long. The flowers, small, white or pink, come in corymbs and bloom in April. The species makes a fine mass of flat foliage (bright green above and paler beneath) for the water-garden. L. H. Bailey describes the plant under *Saxifraga peltata* and says it is: "Hardy in Massachusetts, with slight protection, and a most desirable plant where bold effects are desired".

Petasotes japonica. Its leaves are similarly flat and provide good bold clumps in the water-garden. They are often four feet across and come on thick fleshy stems. The flowers, purplish, are carried in panicles in February. Var. *gigantea* is larger and in rich damp soil reaches a height of six feet. In Japan its stems are cooked and eaten as a vegetable or served, with sugar, as a desert.

Petasites is from *petasos*, a broad-rimmed hat, referring to the large flat leaves.

Phalaris arundinacea variegata, an ornamental Grass known as the Ribbon Grass or Gardener's Garters. The leaves three-quarters of an inch wide, with thin white stripes, are highly decorative in spring. Later the flowering stems go up to a height of from two to five feet and carry small panicles of greenish purple spikelets. A fine Grass for the side of a pool. It likes moist soil and is increased by division.

Phyllostachys are hardy Bamboos; another genus, species of which we grow, is *Arundinaria*. (*See page 108*). Several species of *Phyllostachys* have been described; they are excellent plants for the water-garden and unrivalled for tropical effects.

P. boryana (named in honour of Baron Bory de St. Vincent, 1780—1846, a French traveller and naturalist). It much resembles the famous *P. henonis* in the luxuriant growth of its arching stems. These are green at first, then change to yellow. It is hardly as tall as the other. I saw it used years ago as a companion-plant to the giant Gunnera, both growing near shallow water.

P. castillonis reaches a height of about eight feet in Devon and Cornwall and is much taller in the South of France. Because of the beautiful colouring of the stems, it has been singled out by many gardeners as the choicest member of this family. They are a bright golden yellow and dark green. The leaves vary from two to five inches in length and are three-quarters of an inch wide. They are green and usually striped with yellow and cream. These species, like the others, need a deep rich moist soil.

Polygonum cuspidatum (cuspidate; the leaf coming to a narrow, projecting, often sharp point). A tall, woody perennial plant, sometimes nine feet or more high, which is well adapted for woodland clearings. It looks out of place in a flower-border, although the plant is occasionally used there. It has large ovalish leaves which are conspicuous against the thick red stems; its creamy white flowers are carried in smallish feathery panicles but come in profusion and are beautiful against the foliage.

P. sachalinense (from the Island of Sachalin, East Asia) is similar in habit but larger in its stems and its leaves. A notorious spreader, it should be relegated to a wild spot in the garden where it can be grown with tall vigorous shrubs like the Laurel. The leaves of this *Polygonum* are about twelve inches long and five inches wide. The greenish yellow flowers come in axillary clusters.

The generic name is from a Greek word meaning many-jointed; referring to the swollen nodes.

Polypodium vulgare is the Wall Fern or Wood Fern, a native of Britain and found wild in many temperate parts of the world. The fronds are four to ten inches long and come on stems about half that height. A narrow-leaved, graceful little Fern (evergreen), which assorts well with that woodland creeper *Nepeta hederacea*. (*Described on page 157*).

The varieties are better known in cultivation and appear in most nurserymen's lists. Var.

cambricum (Welsh) has elegant fronds up to two feet in length and are eight inches wide; it is a valuable plant for massing in the woodland.

Hillier lists var. *cornubiense* (of Cornwall), nine inches tall, with fronds cut up into very narrow segments.

These Ferns need a shady place in cool, moist vegetable soil which, however, must be well drained. The three may be grown in pots in a cool greenhouse, their finely divided foliage making an excellent foil to other cool-greenhouse plants such as *Primula sinensis,* P. obconica, etc.

Rheum (from an old Greek name *rha,* rhubarb). The ornamental Rhubarbs are large-leaved foliage plants which will appeal to lovers of big leaves, who haven't room for the giant Gunneras.

R. emodi (of Mt. Emodus, Northern India) is not often seen in our gardens. Its leaves are waved at the margins, ovalish-shaped and copper -coloured. The stems are from five to ten feet long; and the flowers come in upright panicles. It doesn't take up as much space as the big Gunneras, but a good-sized border is needed for it.

R. palmatus has deeply lobed leaves on long

stems and forms a thick mound of foliage from which shoot up the tall flower-stems carrying long large panicles of deep red flowers. A noble plant. Habitat: China.

In the variety *tanguticum*, the leaves are larger and more deeply lobed. I have seen it used in herbaceous borders and on the banks of streams and pools. Like the other Rhubarbs, it needs a good deep moist loam.

The two varieties *atrosanguineum* and 'Bowles' Crimson' have tall, upright crimson flower-panicles which are ideally set off by the deep green flat leaves.

Rheums are used with remarkable effect in semi-woodland at the Savill Gardens.

They like partial shade and benefit much from an annual top dressing of peat or leaf mould.

Any one of the plants mentioned here looks very effective when set on its own against a deeper green background, say, that provided by a Cypress.

Ricinus communis, variously called the Castor-oil Plant; Castor Bean; Palma Christi, grows up to the size of a tree in the tropics, and may get fairly tall in our southern gardens; but around London it seldom goes above three or four feet in height and must be housed during the winter. More often than not it is grown in a pot and stood outside from June till the frosts come.

The large shining green leaves, five- to twelve-lobed, come on long stalks and have a decided exotic look about them; they assort poorly however with most of the ordinary perennials and shrubs we grow in our gardens. In fact it is difficult to find a suitable companion for the plant. It is best (where there is room) to mass half a dozen or more together in a large round bed and aim at some tropical effect. Such a planting would look well on the bank of a pool: here (if the soil were moist and rich enough) some of the Bamboos could be set at the back.

The flowers, male and female, come in panicles and are greenish in colour. From the seeds castor oil is expressed; most of it is produced in India, where the plant is widely cultivated.

A rich well-drained soil is required. The plant is raised from seeds sown indoors in single pots during March; the seedlings are set out at the beginning of June and, where the climate is warm enough, the plants can be left to grow on.

It is very variable, numerous forms of it being offered by different nurseries.

Var. *cambodgensis* has large purplish leaves and blackish stems and branches. Var. *gibsoni* and *sanguineus* both have reddish leaves; and in var. *Zanzibarensis* the bright green leaves have whitish veins.

The generic name is from *ricinus*, a tick. Turner in his *Herbal* (1562) says: "Ricinum is called in English *Palma Christi*, or ticke sede. . . The sede . . . when the huske is of . . . looketh lyke a dogge louse which is called a tyke".

Rodgersia belong to the large-leaved class of foliage plants and like most of these revel in cool moist situations: the woodland or the semi-wild garden, for example.

R. podophylla (*podos*, foot; *phyllon*, leaf; the leaf appearing to resemble a webbed foot). It was the first species to be introduced into cultivation and has leaves, five-foliolate, measuring six to eighteen inches across. The flowers, yellowish white, come in large panicles on long stems in July. A well-grown clump after some years may measure as much as eight or nine feet in diameter. An imposing plant whose leaves are a brownish-red colour, the colour lasting well and taking on a more intense hue in the sun.

A native of Japan; introduced in 1880.

R. aesculifolia (Horse chestnut-like; referring to the leaves). In April this species shoots up through the moist leafy soil in the Savill Gardens, the five radiating leaflets (like those of a Horse chestnut leaf) being of a rich russet-brown colour and coming on long slender stems. It is uncommonly beautiful then, and in summer the flowers, white, come in large clusters on long stems. Habitat: China.

R. pinnata has leaves with five to nine leaflets, which are about six inches long and half as wide; the flowers, red, are carried in a much-branched panicle.

The variety *superba* is superior to it as a garden-plant and has long panicles of rich pink flowers.

Rodgersias need shelter from wind and like a sunny position.

The genus was named in honour of Admiral Edmund John Rodgers, 1812—82, United States Navy. During one of his expeditions to Japan, the species *R. podophylla* was first discovered.

Rumex alpinus is a noble-looking weed indigenous to certain parts of Britain and, of course, rarely planted in gardens. But it is very striking grown in isolation, its ovalish downy leaves, six to twenty-four inches long, showing up in a very striking way. A good choice for the edge of an artificial pool.

Ruta graveolens variegata. A plant which may be seen in the Oxford Botanic Garden. It is an evergreen shrub that has been grown in our gardens since the middle of the sixteenth century and is commonly known as Rue or Herb of Grace. The leaves are glaucous, three to five inches long, Fern-like, the leaflets bordered with white; the flowers, yellow, come in terminal corymbs.

This shrub makes a fine foliage plant all through the year and is valuable in the herbaceous border. It seldom grows taller than three feet; its finely divided leaves are an excellent foil to Delphiniums.

Ordinary loamy soil suits it. Propagate it by cuttings taken in the summer.

The plant is a native of Southern Europe. Hillier lists the type plant. "An evergreen herb, long cultivated for its medicinal properties. The bright yellow flowers contrast well with the glaucous, compound foliage."

Turner states in his *Herbal* (1562): "The juice of Rue is good for the ake of the eares".

Salvia officinalis is the common Sage we grow in the kitchen-garden. Its leaves, grey and furry, and its white woolly stems make it quite a valuable foliage plant for the herbaceous border. But it spreads and becomes untidy unless it is restricted.

The variety *purpurascens* (known as the Purple Sage) has reddish purple leaves and is a popular bedder with many gardeners. Its warm colour is very effective associated with red- or pink-flowered plants. Both Salvias are strongly aromatic.

Most striking of the group is var. *tricolor*, its grey-green leaves, veined with yellow and pink, turning to a velvety rose-red in late summer.

These plants thrive in ordinary garden soil.

Santolina (from *Sanctum linum*, Holy Flax, the popular name of *S. virens*). The best-known species is the Lavender Cotton. *S. chamae-cyparissus* (dwarf cypress-like), the silver-white foliage plant whose leaves are pungently aromatic. In poor sandy soil, the curly looking foliage takes on a whiter hue and clipped back drastically in the spring makes a pretty edging.

The variety *nana* is dwarfer and may be used either as an edging or in rockeries — planted at the base of a rock.

New plants are better than old. I prefer to raise them every year by taking cuttings in summer. The small flower-heads are a hard shade of yellow; they are usually clipped off in their bud stage.

The Cotton Lavender is a native of Southern Europe.

Saxifrage stolonifera (bearing stolons) is commonly known as Mother of Thousands; other names are Roving Sailor and Strawberry Geranium.

It is, or was, better known as a pot-plant than as an alpine for the rockery, where only very occasionally it is to be seen. For it is rather tender and needs a sheltered crevice facing north; planted in poorish sandy soil and adequately protected, it will survive mild frosts.

In the variety *tricolor*, the small round, marbled leaves are exquisitely marked with white and red; but this plant is more tender and does best in a cool greenhouse.

When used in formal bedding schemes, the long flower-stems are cut off.

The species is a native of China and Japan.

The genus *Saxifrage* contains many species

and varieties which are worth growing for their foliage alone. Some of the silver-encrusted ones are particularly lovely. *S. crustata*, whose leaves come in close rosettes (they are silver-edged) is typical.

Scrophularia nodosa variegata is a perennial weed found in our ditches and hedgerows, but nonetheless a good foliage plant for certain places in the garden. It has large green leaves blotched with yellow and cream and is very effective in the semi-wild-garden. The flowers should be pinched out, for they are insignificant; the foliage is doubly attractive without them.

Sedum acre is the Common Stonecrop, whose thread-like stems covered with tiny juice leaves creep over brick-work and arid patches of soil where nothing else will grow. The variety *aureum*, with golden-yellow leaves in spring, is much more striking and often used as an edging-plant in formal beds and borders.

But there are no species or varieties to touch *S. spathuliolium purpureum* for beauty of foliage. (The leaves are spatulate — having the shape of a spatula — succulent and plum purplish in colour.) The plant forms rosettes, which in time spread out on runner-stems and make mats of grey-purple foliage with an exquisite Plum-like bloom. The colour varies according to the situation and the soil in which the plant is grown. In a sandy loamy medium and in full sun, it is at its best. Too much shade, or too starved a site, tends to destroy the rich glaucous colouring. The rosettes measure two inches across on well-developed specimens.

Sedum is from *sedeo*, to sit, many of the plants "sitting" on, or attaching themselves to, stonework. Both the species described here do, spreading equally well on vertical or on horizontal rock.

Sempervivum arachnoideum (cobwebby; covered with cobweb-like white hairs). The Cobweb Houseleek, with thrives in the driest places. Anybody can grow it; even those who haven't a garden. For it is often planted in a pot or a pan and needs an ordinary light sandy loam. The two Sedums described above can also be grown in pots. And the three together in a flat earthenware pan make a charming trio.

This Houseleek spreads by means of its rosettes, the longest being about one inch in diameter; the tops of the tiny leaflets are connected by soft white cobwebby hairs. The

172

plant will grow on a vertical rock-face (set a single rosette in a crevice of leafy sandy soil and let it spread). The flowers, pinkish red, come on stems about four inches high. In exceptionally dry arid places, they are not freely produced; but the foliage is always beautiful.

The species is found wild in the Pyrenees.

The generic name is from the Latin *semper vivo*, to live for ever.

Senecio laxifolius (loose, not compact leaves). It is *S. greyii* to most people and still appears under this name in catalogues. But *S. greyii* is a different plant and rather tender.

S. laxifolius makes a spreading plant often eight feet across and is seldom more than three or four feet high. The leaves, ovalish, are about two inches long and half as wide, grey-green above and conspicuously white and woolly beneath. The branclets and flower-stems are similarly covered. In summer the brilliant yellow Daisy-flowers transform the shrub completely. I prefer to cut the buds off before they open — and I notice this is done in many gardens.

It thrives in ordinary loamy soils and needs full sun.

Propagate it by cuttings, which strike readily

out of doors.

Habitat: New Zealand.

S. cineraria (ash- or grey-coloured) A grey-silver velvety species which I cannot get to stand the winter in South Bucks. It is much less popular as a garden-plant than the other species and appears to be used mostly (at least around London) as a silver foliage plant for formal bedding. It is kept down to about twelve inches and, with its dense covering of white down, is singularly attractive in Carpet-beds. It is one of the Dusty Millers and occasionally grown in a pot.

Spinacia oleracea. The Spinach is grown primarily as a vegetable; but one finds it sometimes in the herbaceous border, its long, puckered, fresh green leaves providing a delightful contrast with the flowers. Seed should be sown where the plant or plants are to grow. Deep rich loam is best for it.

The generic name is from *spina*, prickles; some of the fruits are of a prickly nature.

Oleracea: growing in a cultivated place; referring to its use as a vegetable.

Stacys lanata (woolly) is popularly known as Lamb's Tongue. The leaves are soft, furry, oblong-shaped (perhaps thought to be tongue-shaped) and of a beautiful silver-grey colour.

The plant seldom goes above a foot in height and gives its best results, I think, in a mass (though many people do not care for its spikes of staring purplish flowers). If they are cut off, it can be used as a silver foliage plant — in bedding-out or in the herbaceous border. It prospers in any ordinary loamy soil and is increased by division.

Habitat: Caucasus to Persia. It was introduced into England towards the end of the eighteenth century.

Thalictrum speciosissimum (very showy: the leaves are beautifully formed, rather like a large Maidenhair-fern, and glaucous). The species is often described in catalogues under *T. glaucum*, the epithet describing the foliage. When the tufts of pale yellow flowers fade, they should be cut off; the plant stands then, with its conspicuously lovely glaucous leaves, the equal of any other foliage plant we may choose to grow in the herbaceous border. It is an excellent foil to flowers like Delphiniums and Lilies. Grow it in a good loamy soil and propagate it by division — the plant benefits from lifting every third year.

Thymus pseudolanuginosus (resembling the species *T. lanuginosus*). Our plant still appears under the second name in many catalogues and is commonly known as the Woolly-leaved Thyme. It is refreshingly and sweetly fragrant, and a mat of it in spring has a pleasing silky greenish grey appearance — the tiny leaves, crowded on long creeping stems, have silky hairs on both sides. These are most pronounced when new growth begins in April; the plant is then at its best. I must confess I've never seen it in bloom; some specimens do have a few scattered pink flowers; but it is unusual to see them.

It spreads quickly in light sandy loam and in sunny places and, although it is considered too invasive for the Alpine Lawn, it is used there by some gardeners for the sake of its scent, which smells strongest when the plant is touched — and especially when it is trodden on.

In the rockery it makes a sheet of silky foliage; I like to see it covering part of the face of a retaining-wall.

T. serpyllum (with Thyme-like leaves) is the Wild Thyme, of which there are many garden forms, all useful for carpeting in sunny places. Many have rich purplish flowers: var. *coccineus*, for instance; one offered by the Clarence Elliot Nurseries, 'Cloth of Gold', has green foliage in winter, which is golden coloured all through the summer.

Thymes are easily propagated by division in spring or autumn and should be clipped over after they have flowered to keep them neat and compact.

Tulipa greigii. A wild Tulip from Turkistan which is naturally grown for its flowers, these being bright scarlet, yellow and blotched with black. The leaves, about eight inches long and half as wide, glaucous and wonderfully marked with purplish red specks, vie with those of any of the smaller Hostas; they are much more exotic-looking, though not so numerous, and by the summer are past their best. But while they last, they are among the most decorative of the glaucous, broad leaves that can be seen in our gardens.

This Tulip is often protected by a cloche, for the flowers may be damaged by frost and rain. Half a dozen plants set in a clump at the front of a border give an extraordinarily beautiful foliage-effect in late April and May. There is a hybrid raised from the species, viz. 'Margaret Herbst', which has very striking mottled leaves.

Veratum album (white; referring to the flowers). In its young state, about April, the plant, a foot high, resembles a Hosta; the lowest leaves, pleated and oblong-shaped, are twelve inches long and about six inches wide. But the plant soon grows tall, the stalkless leaves coming up the stems and making a striking foliage plant up to three feet or so high. The whitish-green flowers are carried in dense racemes in July but are not particularly decorative.

V. nigrum (blackish; the flowers are a blackish purple colour). Its broad leaves — the largest, twelve inches long by eight inches wide — are, like those of the other species, beautifully pleated and the plant's chief attraction. It goes up to a height of four feet or more; the purplish star-shaped flowers bloom in June. Both these species are natives of Southern Europe and Siberia.

V. viride (greenish). The flowers are yellowish green and, as in the others, less attractive than the leaves; these are about a foot long at the base of the plant and become increasingly smaller towards the top.

The Veratums are an excellent choice for the woodland-garden, provided the sun can reach them; but their foliage is of great value in the flower-border. They want a position where they show up well.

They thrive in rich leafy soils and are propagated by division.

Verbascum. Many perennial kinds are offered by the nurseries. Some species are found growing in open sunny spots in the countryside and, with their large felty leaves and long spikes of bright yellow flowers, are as decorative as the Foxglove.

The plants are popularly known as Mulleins; and *V. nigrum* is the Dark Mullein, which one occasionally finds growing wild. Its leaves are heart-shaped, slightly downy beneath and very handsome. The flower-spikes are yellow.

V. olympicum (of Greece) is a finer foliage plant, its large rosettes of grey-felted leaves making a wonderful show, especially when the plant stands well to the front of a flower-border. It reaches a height of six feet, the flower-panicles, yellow, branching out from the base.

Veronica × andersonii variegata. This hybrid, evergreen shrub may be seen in one of the foliage-borders at Oxford and is remarkable for the variegation of its leaves; they are small and narrow, blotched with white and pink above, and some are deep carmine beneath. It was a popular foliage plant for formal bedding at one time, but is rarely used as such nowadays. The plant does well in a good loamy soil and, as it is rather on the tender side, should be given a sheltered spot.

Vinca is the Periwinkle which we sometimes come across in our woods, where it grows as an undergrowth among trees; it is a dainty plant with its small blue-purple star-shaped flowers. It succeeds in practically any soil and spreads quickly. There are two variegated forms worth growing in the wild-garden or the woodland, viz. *V. major variegata*, whose leaves are blotched creamy white; and *V. minor variegata*, with yellow variegations.

Yucca (from the West Indian word *yuca*, which is the manihot or cassava, the name being erroneously applied to the Genus *Yucca*). They have sword-shaped leaves, which are mostly tipped with a sharp point. The foliage is thick and leathery and decidedly exotic-looking, which makes the plants very suitable for sub-tropical effects. And they should be massed, for they are most imposing then. When they bloom, they give a magnificent show of, usually, creamy white pendulous bell-like flowers, which come in tall spikes. In some districts, particularly in the north, they are shy flowerers; but their foliage is evergreen and strong and pleasing all the winter. I have come across specimens in gardens near London which bloom only at intervals of several years. (*V. gloriosa* is seldom a free bloomer). In one garden the deficiency had been made good by planting as a groundwork amongst a group of this species the soft velvety silver-white foliage-plant *Senecio cineraria*. This was one of the most striking associations. I have ever seen. The contrast between the free woolly silver foliage and the sharp, erect, dark green Yucca leaves was astonishing; furthermore the Senecios had a softening effect on the hard formal leaves of the other plants. Had these been in flower, the effect would have been doubly beautiful.

Yucca glauca is one of the easiest of all the species to grow. Its glaucous leaves, two feet long and half an inch wide, shoot up from the main stem, which is scarcely visible; and the greenish white pendulous flowers come in erect racemes about three feet tall.

Y. filamentosa (thread-like; referring to the numerous marginal threads of the leaves). A species as hardy as the other and perhaps more

181

often grown in our gardens, and one which normally flowers freely even in its young state. The leaves are about two and a half feet long and from one inch to four inches broad. They have curly white threads on the margins, come to a point; are slightly glaucous, and the outer ones are recurved. The flowers, yellowish white, are carried in erect racemes from three to six feet tall. A fine plant (with fine growth) for massing. In the variety *variegata*, the leaves are margined and striped with yellow. Both species are natives of the South Eastern United States.

Yuccas need all the sun they can get and a perfectly drained sandy loam. They are best propagated by rhizome cuttings: pieces two or three inches long should be placed in sandy loam in gentle heat. They may also be raised from seeds and by offsets.

Zebrina (from the Portuguese word *zebra*; the name refers to the stripes on the leaves). *Z. pendula* is our last foliage plant; it seems to have become one of the best known for pot-culture and to have ousted the Aspidistra; for where that majestic plant once stood, there is now usually a pot of this very attractive trailing-plant. Wandering Jew is one of its popular names, and it is often referred to as a *Trades-cantia*, *T. color* or *T. zebrina*.

The leaves are about two inches long and one inch across and come on fleshy jointed stems, which trail over pots or over flower-baskets and show off the delightful silvery white and purplish colours to best advantage. (The undersides are purplish red.)

It is very effective used as an edging to a formal bed, but must be lifted before the frosts come; and it makes an uncommonly beautiful trailer in the rockery, but must not be put out before June.

Z. pendula needs a sandy leafy soil and full sun — the stronger the sunlight, the better the colouring of the foliage.

For edging a formal bed a good number of plants will be wanted and they should be set fairly close together in two rows nine inches apart. It is an easy matter to raise the plants: cuttings root very readily and will do so out of doors during the summer.

A foliage border as a feature of a garden is rarely seen. There is one at Hampton Court (it was designed in 1953) and has as a background a hedge of pleached Limes and clipped Yew.

I was interested to see in it some of the plants mentioned here, viz. *Arundinaria, Coleus, Dahlia* 'Bishop of Llandaff', *Echeverias, Iresines, Senecio laxifolius* and *Veronica* × *andersonii.*

635.975
B294f

LARGE TYPE EDITION